Moral Agents

Moral Agents

Eight Twentieth-Century American Writers

Edward Mendelson

NEW YORK REVIEW BOOKS

New York

THIS IS A NEW YORK REVIEW BOOK
PUBLISHED BY THE NEW YORK REVIEW OF BOOKS
435 Hudson Street, New York NY 10014
www.nyrb.com

Library of Congress Cataloging-in-Publication Data

Mendelson, Edward, author.
Moral agents : Eight Twentieth-Century American writers /
by Edward Mendelson.
pages cm. —
Includes bibliographical references.
ISBN 978-1-59017-776-1 (hardback)
1. American literature—20th century—History and criticism.
2. Literature and history—
United States—History—20th century. 3. United States—Intellectual
life—20th century. I. Title.
PS221.M4 2015
810.9'005—dc23

2014029155

ISBN 978-1-59017-776-1
Available as an electronic book; ISBN 978-1-59017-806-5

Printed in the United States of America on acid-free paper
1 3 5 7 9 10 8 6 4 2

For
Robert B. Silvers

Contents

Preface

THE DEDICATION OF this book is literally accurate. I wrote these essays, in their original form, because Robert B. Silvers commissioned them for *The New York Review of Books*. My knowledge that he would read them provided much of the challenge and pleasure of writing them.

After completing two or three, I realized that they were beginning to shape themselves into a book, and I wrote the rest with something like this book in mind. In rewriting and rearranging, I have dropped almost everything in the originals that served as a review of a biography, edition, or critical study, and I have added much new material. Some of the chapters weave together material from two separate essays about the same author into a single narrative, and the introduction includes some paragraphs adapted from yet another piece I wrote for the *Review*. Every page has benefited from the vast learning, sharp eye, and profound good sense of Edwin Frank at New York Review Books.

All writers maintain a list of readers, not all of them still living, whom they most hope to please. At the head of my list, in alphabetical order, are David Bromwich, Barbara J. Fields, the shade of the late Frank Kermode, Cheryl Mendelson, and James Mendelson.

Introduction

THIS IS A book about writers, morality, and power. It tells the story of eight twentieth-century novelists, poets, and critics who, in addition to practicing their craft, seized for themselves the power and authority to shape American literary culture. Some exercised their power as public intellectuals whose writings influenced the national agenda. Others worked unobtrusively as editors who imposed their taste on an audience that was largely unaware of them. All had mixed feelings about their own power, and each confronted moral tests and temptations that were inseparable from it. Each of the eight chapters tells the story of one writer's response to those tests.

The word "moral" embarrasses otherwise intelligent readers who imagine it has something to do prohibitions, social codes, or supernatural decrees. In fact morality concerns the effect of one's thoughts and acts, for good or ill, on others and oneself. It is a matter of the inner logic of actions and consequences, not of precepts and rules. It is descriptive, not prescriptive, in the way that the laws of thermodynamics are descriptive; however, one's actions may be guided, in part, by an understanding of morality in much the same way that a knowledge of the basic laws of physics may persuade you that it is preferable to walk down the stairs than to jump out the window. As in most realms of action, definitions tend to falsify; morality is a matter of what one does, not what one is. The clearest statement of this view of morality is Thucydides' history of the Peloponnesian War. As Thucydides portrays them, acts of vengeance, capital punishment, and imperialist war are all self-defeating, not because they are punished by fate or the gods, but because they bring about their own failure, always foreseeable by those who have some moral sense, always denied by those who imagine themselves exempt from morality's logic. All societies try to translate morality, with varying degrees of unsuccess, into codes of law and conduct, but those codes inevitably lack the inner logic and coherence of morality itself.

A few years ago I wrote a book titled *The Things That Matter,* about seven novels from *Frankenstein* to *Between the Acts.* All five authors that I wrote about in that book were women. All eight authors in this one are men. The choice of authors in each case has nothing to do with any homogenizing fantasy that women and men have different essential qualities, or that one category is inherently deeper and wiser about one or another aspect of experience. In both these books, the selection of authors deliberately reflects nineteenth- and twentieth-century social realities that were the product of stereotyping and prejudice.

The unifying theme of *The Things That Matter* was individuality, and its subject matter was the unique inner life of individual persons. All five of the novelists in that book—Mary Shelley, Emily and Charlotte Brontë, George Eliot, and Virginia Woolf—knew they would be stereotyped as women writers, resented the stereotype, and rebelled against it by insisting on the unique meaning and value of individual life. This new book is a sequel to the earlier one, and it has a double focus on the inner life and the life of the political and cultural marketplace. Its subject matter is the effect of power on both private and public experience, and it describes a specific literary culture in which power was available only to men. Women writers from Katherine Anne Porter through Mary McCarthy to Sylvia Plath could be celebrated for their womanly insights but only if they held back from social and political subjects reserved for men—although an anthropologist like Margaret Mead was tolerated for her knowledge of powerless cultures far from the American empire. (The same tolerance extended to child psychologists and other experts in powerlessness.) One recurring episode in this book is the hate-campaign mounted against Hannah Arendt after she discredited many conventional pieties in *Eichmann in Jerusalem* in 1963, a campaign that would have been far more cautious had the book been written by a man.

This book, like its predecessor, is concerned with individual persons, but it focuses on the conflicts between the inward, intimate private lives of its eight authors and the lives they led in public, the choices they continually made between wearing a mask and exposing their face. Some wore masks of exemplary rectitude, others wore equally artificial masks of wickedness, but all were troubled by the discordance between a mask and a face.

The oldest of these eight authors, Lionel Trilling, was born in 1905, the youngest, Frank O'Hara, in 1926. All knew most or all of the others. The first to publish a book with a commercial press was W. H. Auden, in 1930; the last was Norman Mailer, in 2007. For much of their lives, all lived and worked in New York, the capital of twentieth-century American literary and artistic culture. Dwight Macdonald edited his magazine *Politics,* with its worldwide influence, from his apartment in New York; William Maxwell shaped the dominant style of American novels and stories from his office as fiction editor of *The New Yorker*; W. H. Auden set the dominant tone of mid-century American poetry from his Lower East Side flat where he edited the Yale Series of Younger Poets; Frank O'Hara molded fashions in American painting from his office at the Museum of

Modern Art. The apparent exception was Saul Bellow, who spent only a dozen years in New York—where he wrote his best work—but Bellow seems to have left the city for the same motives of power that drew others toward it: he knew he could dominate the culture of Chicago in a way that no one writer could manage in New York.

These eight chapters serve as a highly selective cultural history of almost a century of American life. It is not a history of themes and issues, but of individual writers finding their own unique ways of responding to a shared world. Almost all recent thought about history and literature takes one side or another in a pervasive but unstated argument about what it means to be a person: whether one shapes one's own life through individual choices, which may be conscious or unconscious but are primarily one's own; or whether one's life is shaped from outside by large impersonal forces of culture, history, gender, ethnicity, class, archetype, or myth. Both sides of the argument of course are correct—everyone is shaped by both inner impulses and outward forces—but it matters which side of the argument you believe in most.

If you think the most decisive facts about human beings are their choices, you also focus your intellectual and emotional attention on their individual freedom, on their ability to change over time, on the ways they exist as changing personal histories rather than as unchanging social or psychological types, and on the equal and unequal relations they have with other individual persons. You approach the world differently from those who think that what is most decisive in life is the shaping force of culture or history, or an ethnic or sexual category that people seem to fit into. Those who think this latter way tend to focus on their sense that they are driven by powers they cannot control. In their vocabulary and syntax they tend to be passive objects, and their tone is the inevitable melancholy of unfreedom. They seem preoccupied less with their individual relations with other persons than with their greater or lesser status in a cultural or social marketplace; they measure themselves (the academic phrase is "situate themselves") along a scale or in a diagram.

Many books about the literature and culture of a historical period tend to treat individual authors as more or less interchangeable voices speaking for the culture a whole. (In another academic phrase, they perform "cultural work.") In such a book, each chapter focuses on one common issue or theme, and various authors are quoted as typifying one aspect of a collective view of that theme. This approach, I think, distorts the reality of everyone's experience. Everyone filters historical events or cultural trends through private experience and private emotions. The outbreak of war makes one person anxious or terrified, but makes another excited or exhilarated. A great historical cataclysm may be experienced, not as newspapers and histories report it, but as a welcome distraction from someone's psychological complexities, or as an unwelcome intrusion on someone's comfortable egoism.

All these eight writers responded to great events, among them the Great Depression, the rise of Soviet Communism, the Second World War, the atomic bomb, the Cold War, the civil rights movement, the war in Vietnam, and the upheavals of the 1960s and after. But these events did not make them think or react in any consistent or conventional way. Like everyone, they were provoked—not compelled—by the events around them. In Thomas Pynchon's *The Crying of Lot 49*, the heroine Oedipa Maas tries to convince herself that someone acted in an unpredictable way because "something must have happened," some external event caused him to act as he did. Another character responds doubtfully: "You think a man's mind is a pool table?"

American culture has always been troubled by the question of what it means to be an individual person. Two great myths have combined to shape American thinking about this question since the early nineteenth century.

One myth holds that you can only become yourself by insisting on being alone, unencumbered by entangling alliances, relationships, or obligations. This is an idea shared by writers as various as Mark Twain—Huck Finn lights out for the territory to avoid being adopted and civilized—and Henry James, whose heroes and heroines choose the lonely integrity of honor over the corrupting compromises of love. The distance between the Jamesian variety of this myth and the up-to-date variety that celebrates the outlaw-hero is not large, despite their extreme differences of manner and tone.

The second myth offers a solution to the loneliness inflicted by the first. It holds that the only relations worth having with other people are not the corrupting individual relations between Huck Finn and Aunt Sally, or between Lambert Strether and Maria Gostrey in *The Ambassadors*, but those in which individual selves dissolve into something anonymous and collective. This myth is beautiful and moving in Walt Whitman's poetry; less so in twentieth-century fantasies about everyone's supposed need to live within a collective ethnic or sexual "identity."

Some varieties of this second myth hold that everyone is already defined from birth by some collective ethnic or sexual identity, and that one can only become oneself by embracing that identity; the most pernicious such myth served as the primary justification for slavery. Ernest Hemingway spent his life divided between his public adherence to a myth about manliness and his private revolt against it. Four of the authors in this book were born into Jewish families, but they all thought differently at different times—and spoke differently in public and private—about the effect that their origins had, or ought to have had, on their lives.

In the American novel, on the whole, the goal of the plot is the liberation of the hero (Natty Bumppo, Captain Ahab, Jake Barnes, Janie Crawford) from other people's values and demands, an escape from all relations of the kind in which individual persons find some accommodation with each other. In the British novel, the goal, whether or not any character achieves it, is more often a liberation from loneliness into marriage and family, a triumph that the hero (Jane Eyre, David Copperfield, Dorothea Brooke, Leopold Bloom) can achieve only with the help of others.* The fantasy that someone might write the Great American Novel has no counterpart elsewhere in the world, because only writers who were Americans have imagined literature as a competition in which one book or writer can dominate all others, or have imagined that one writer can encompass a whole culture—that a single individual can be the voice of a collective national identity.

The mid-twentieth century was an era when American public intellectuals—such as Reinhold Niebuhr, Jacques Barzun, and John Kenneth Galbraith—appeared regularly on the cover of *Time* magazine.† The American public intellectual, unlike his counterparts in Britain and France, could serve as a reassuring secular spiritual adviser—Lionel Trilling's public role when he became famous around 1950—rather than a despairing prophet in the nineteenth-century British mold of Matthew Arnold, Thomas Carlyle, or John Ruskin—or the French models of the literary *monstre sacré* like André Gide

---

* The only generalization I would dare to make about the French, German, Italian, or Russian novel is that they often differ from both the American and English model by liberating their hero from a personal relation into an institutional one, from the arms of a tempter into the arms of the church or the state (Stendhal's Fabrice, Balzac's Vautrin).

† Of the eight writers in this book, only Norman Mailer appeared on the cover of *Time*; the magazine had W. H. Auden's portrait painted for a planned cover story, but it was vetoed because, Tennessee Williams having recently appeared on the cover, an editor didn't want to honor yet another homosexual.

and Jean-Paul Sartre or the palace insider like André Malraux. In England, T. S. Eliot made himself a guiding public intellectual in the American manner, but he was able to do so only because he shared in the lonely, isolating ambition special to Americans.

By the early twenty-first century, the American public intellectual had largely disappeared, surviving only in an academic shadow world where conferences are held about the role that public intellectuals might perform again someday. One theme of this book is the double life that the twentieth-century American public intellectuals could not avoid living. Torn between the simplifying demands of their public role and the complex realities of their private feelings, they either endured that division, or they escaped it by renouncing the falsehoods that their admirers insisted on hearing. Even those who escaped were scarred by the experience. Late in life, W. H. Auden gave readings after which, more than once, someone in the audience complained that he was no longer "leading us" as he did in the 1930s— while Auden stared straight ahead, ashamed that he had once made it possible for those who wanted a leader to imagine that he was one.

Each of the eight writers in this book knew that he enjoyed superior intellectual and artistic gifts; each was tempted by the thought that his gifts made him morally superior, that he was qualified and obliged to lead others. Another theme of this book is that, although the leader-figure is always a fantasy, wisdom and knowledge are real—and can be shared only among equals. The whole book is a study in that kind of sharing and in the ways in which a few writers, after many misjudgments and missteps, managed to achieve it.

I

SAGE: LIONEL TRILLING

I.

WHEN LIONEL TRILLING's first book of essays, *The Liberal Imagination,* appeared in 1950, it sold seventy thousand hardback copies. Over the next decade it sold hundreds of thousands more in paperback, and set the agenda for intellectual life in the United States in much the same way that Matthew Arnold and T. S. Eliot had set it in Britain. Trilling was an English professor at Columbia, a specialist in nineteenth- and twentieth-century novels and poetry, who became an international celebrity. For the first and last time, a literature professor enjoyed public eminence and adulation of a kind unimaginable for intellectuals today, and reserved even then typically for an economist like John Kenneth Galbraith or a scientist like Jonas Salk.

Trilling wrote about American culture in a way that was both critical and comforting, and that spoke to the deepest anxieties of the age. Many of his readers—they tended to be thoughtful, educated, more or less liberal in outlook—had been sustained in the 1930s by the moral clarity of the class struggle and in much of the 1940s by the moral urgency of a war against Hitler that ended in triumph. By the early 1950s all this had changed. A cold war between two nuclear-armed superpowers could be won by neither; American culture and American arms now had vast international powers without a clear sense of purpose. Trilling, more fluently and persuasively than anyone else, clarified the mutual entanglements of the collective life of politics and culture and individual private lives. His prose was lucid and urbane, never straying from the reality of mixed feelings and ambiguous purposes into simple pieties and exhortations. He was an establishment figure—professorial, pipe-smoking, with an air of dignified sadness—whose every essay questioned the established order and brought to light its unacknowledged, self-defeating motives.

He was a quietly dominating figure whose reign over literary culture was secure because it was so evidently just. He had no partisan agenda; he played no favorites. He was sensible, sensitive, and reassuring in his chastened emergence from 1930s radicalism and in his nuanced Freudianism. He was never doctrinaire. Liberal politics and psychoanalytic insights, in his hands, offered tentative and subtle ways of understanding the complexities and contradictions of public and private life. When he recommended one or another side of the vexed social and literary questions he wrote about, he did so only after he had explored the motives and meanings of all other sides. His essays served as a form of national therapy. His essay about Henry James's 1886 novel about revolutionary politics, *The Princess Casamassima,* like most of his essays in *The Liberal Imagination,* was also a quietly persuasive parable: it educated his readers away from the simple political certainties of the 1930s and toward the difficult complexities of "ambiguity and error" that they must learn to accept if they hoped to fulfill their generous liberal intentions.

The recurring theme of his work was the conflict between the anarchic energies that drive much of modern literature and art and a society that must repress those energies in the service of rationality and justice. He provoked a minor scandal when he spoke about that conflict, not in one of his ruminative essays, but in a speech at a ceremony honoring an author who embodied it. To celebrate Robert Frost's eighty-fifth birthday, his publishers held a dinner at the Waldorf-Astoria with Trilling, America's most famous critic, as speaker. His speech revealed what Frost's public image had kept secret: that the Frost treasured by readers as a "tutelary genius" was a myth, that the real Frost was "a terrifying poet" who portrayed "a terrifying universe" in poems warmed only by "the energy with which emptiness is perceived."* This seemed a momentary lapse from Trilling's courteous urbanity, but his private—and still mostly unpublished—journals make clear that he was able to see through the mask of the tutelary Robert Frost because he himself lived behind a tutelary mask that he had created for himself many years earlier. His own nihilistic despair was as deep as Frost's, but he concealed it in his private journals— hoping, or half-hoping, that they would be published after his death.

Trilling's strength as a critic was not the product of the sober urbanity for which he was celebrated but his inward experience of the unrepressed, anarchic daemonic energy that, he imagined, set modern art in opposition to modern culture and made the modern artist a dangerous and destructive force. In public, he spoke with the moral authority of a critic who serves society and its virtues by exposing and criticizing the amoral energies of the artist who, indifferent to his fellow-citizens, only "serves his daemon and his subject." Trilling warned repeatedly against the seductive powers of "the fierce, the assertive, the personally militant." He never explained that the subjects of his first two books, *Matthew Arnold* (1939) and *E. M. Forster*

---

* Trilling's speech unleashed a denunciation of him in the *New York Times Book Review*, endorsed a few weeks later by a dozen furious letter-writers. Trilling wrote a letter of apology to Frost, who replied graciously that no apology was needed; he had enjoyed being surprised by what Trilling had to say.

(1943), were the models he chose for his life: the two greatest English writers who had each suppressed their fiercely destructive daemon by renouncing or abandoning their art.

In his private journals Trilling acknowledged the hidden daemonic impulse that drove his public career, his "character-drive to an Olympian or royal position." He also kept recording an impulse, which he never obeyed, to reveal his "sense of the necessity of repudiating the character of public virtue"; "my intense disgust with my official and public self, my growing desire to repudiate it." From the privacy of his journals he observed his public self with ironic disdain:

> Interesting that I should lately have been attacking the charismatic tendencies of our literature, when it is perhaps just the charismatic personalities [Ernest Hemingway, D. H. Lawrence] that I long for.

He kept returning to the crossroads where, as he put it in his journals, "the academic and the men of genius and real originality" choose between forking paths. He resolved each time to choose the heroic path, "to make a full attempt toward 'genius,'" to pursue his true artistic calling as a novelist. Then, although he began many novels and published one, he kept retreating into despairing academic dignity.

He was burdened by his "continuing sense that wickedness—or is it my notion of courage—is essential for creation." Much of the misery recorded in his later journals resulted from his sense that his courage had failed, that he had disguised that failure behind the virtuous mask of his criticism. But he never fully renounced his impulse toward creation. With their latinate diction and Jamesian syntax, his essays announce their calm disinterested wisdom, but Trilling himself observed—having seen it in himself—that "the more a writer takes pain with his work to remove from it the personal and subjective, the more . . . he will express his true unconscious."

His prose unobtrusively refutes its stated commitment to enlightenment, sometimes through quick covert glimpses of chaos and darkness, sometimes through a style that ripens into fierce self-parody at its most affirming moments. "Between the university and reality there now exists the happiest, most intimate relation," he wrote straight-facedly in the preface to *Beyond Culture* (1965), a book that proceeded to explore their mutual alienation. Trilling's ironies were sharpest when he used the word "happy" and its variants, and a persistent theme of his journals is the way in which university professors, far from enjoying a happy relation with reality, were psychologically and socially isolated from it. His colleagues at Columbia, he believed, neither perceived reality nor saw any reason why they should want an intimate relation with it. At Harvard too, where he was briefly tempted by a job offer, the professors "have no real sense of reality"—but they at least "believe they should have." He had been wise to refuse Harvard's offer, he concluded, because his colleagues there would have tried to look behind his mask, while at Columbia, where no one cared about reality, he would be left alone.

No academic critic matched Trilling's power to make a nuanced synthesis of literature, culture, politics, and psychology in a single essay. Trilling's colleague Jacques Barzun used the word "visions" to describe the idiosyncratic form that Trilling developed for putting together in one very short statement the intellectual, social and spiritual elements he had perceived.

These—I will not say capsules, because that sounds mechanical, but I may call them visions—resembled in effect the rose window of a cathedral. He was so adept at creating such summaries . . . that once in a while I doubted some of their contents and wanted to shout, "Evidence, please!" like a heckler at a public meeting.

Trilling's strongest essays are in two movements. First, a long fugal adagio winds its way plausibly and convincingly through the sources and details of the novel he is writing about: the moral judgments in *Emma,* the political insights of *The Princess Casamassima.* Then a brief soaring presto praises the novelist for virtues that exist only in Trilling's visions: he proclaims Jane Austen an idyllic visionary; he finds "perfect equilibrium" at the heart of James's "imagination of love." Equilibrium is Trilling's sole hope for escape from his inner conflict between willfulness and justice, and he ends his essay on James in an ecstatic hymn to "perfect ambivalence," a love that desires nothing, that comprehends "civilized life and...transcends it." Trilling's other name for this transcendent love was "moral realism." His authority was so great that only a few grumblers complained that his hymn of praise for the equilibrium of *The Princess Casamassima* was contradicted by what James actually wrote. Instead of writing the novels he wanted to write, Trilling wrote fictions about other people's novels and made them seem like truth.

In practically all his essays Trilling invoked morality. He usually meant by "morality" a suppression of the will's impulsive wickedness, not an action toward some moral good. Morality for him was always negative, a renunciation or restraint of one's own desire and will. In public, what he valued most in books was the refuge offered by "the moral intelligence of art" against "the panic and emptiness which make their onset when the will is tired from its own excess." Diana Trilling wrote about her husband's "conscience, or perhaps I mean his stern self-prohibitions," but Trilling thought of them instead as defenses. In the depths of his thought, morality and self-preservation were two names for the same renunciation of the will. "That the self may be preserved by the negation of its own energies," by suppressing its self-creating daemon, was the paradox at the heart of his criticism: the self preserves itself by suppressing itself. "Life is nothing unless sacrificial."

II.

Trilling was born in New York in 1905. His father was a Polish Jew who had emigrated to America. Lionel's mother was born in London; her parents were Polish Jews who had emigrated first to England, then to America.* His parents kept kosher but were otherwise minimally observant and celebrated both Hanukkah and Christmas. His mother read biographies and classic novels. When Lionel was six, she told him he was going to earn his doctorate at Oxford.

Trilling went from Columbia College to Columbia Graduate School because, he said, he wanted to write novels, and a modern novelist needed learning. In 1927 he met Diana Rubin, the Radcliffe-educated daughter of prosperous secular Jews. Defying convention, they secretly became lovers six months before they married in 1929. In 1930 Diana developed severe and disfiguring hyperthyroidism that required surgery, followed by years of disabling panic attacks and phobias—she could not bear to be above the ground floor, for example—that called for Trilling's constant care. She began her writing

---

* During his lifetime it was widely but mistakenly assumed that Trilling had changed his name to something gentile-sounding. "Wassertrilling" and "Trilling" were common Jewish names around Moravia, and his Anglophile mother seems to have chosen "Lionel" for him.

career in 1941 when Trilling recommended her to the left-wing weekly *The Nation,* and soon became famous as a sharp-tongued reviewer and essayist whose work appeared everywhere, from literary quarterlies to fashion magazines, but who never wrote a book of her own until after her husband's death.

They were the best-known literary couple of their time, in public a model of balanced opposites, Diana embodying passionate energy (she edited a selection from D. H. Lawrence), Lionel embodying sober decorum (he wrote a book about E. M. Forster). She was notoriously ferocious to the young and vulnerable, but her anger was so operatically extravagant, so lacking in personal malice, that many people she attacked were surprised to find themselves loving her as a friend.

In private, the balance was more precarious. Trilling repeatedly noted in his journal the "resentment so central to our marriage," his "anger and resentment at D[iana]." Together, they were emotionally "violent beyond what anybody might guess, seeing us in our character of lovers of amenity, etc." She wrote in her memoir, *The Beginning of the Journey* (1993), that she "had indeed done Lionel injury." The "phobias and the many worrisome illnesses of my young womanhood robbed him of the carefreeness of youth."

"Lionel taught me to think," she wrote. "I taught him to write." Reviewers ridiculed her claim, but it seems to have been true, though only partly in the way she thought. In the unique circumstances of their marriage, in the sacrifices Trilling felt obliged to make, he discovered the great themes of his criticism: "the pain and suffering that the moral life entails," his stoic refusal of willful "wickedness," his sense of sexuality as an escape from culture, his despair over every possible course of action—and in reaction to all these, the visions of ideal equanimity that he found or invented in Austen and James.

Trilling's imagination was dialectical; he could not argue a point without finding arguments for its antithesis. Diana Trilling's memoir plausibly suggests a private source for this habit of mind: as he developed his courtly and judicious public persona, she served as his inescapable dialectical opposite by turning caustic and explosive. His mature essays almost invariably hovered between antithetical positions—the claims of civilization, the force of instinct—while hers delivered summary judgments against literary offenders. As he became Socrates, she became Xantippe.

Before he married, Trilling wrote his essays and reviews in a tone of thin-lipped detachment. Then, for a few years afterward, he adopted a new, sometimes fiercely intense tone, a passionate response to literature and culture—when he was in fact writing in a clandestine way about the intimate antipathies of his marriage. A few months after marrying Diana, he wrote in a book review:

> There is only one way to accept America and that is in hate; one must be close to one's land, passionately close in some way or other, and the only way to be close to America is to hate it; it is the only way to love America.

By 1936 he had built a reputation as a sophisticated left-leaning reviewer, but he was stalled on his Columbia Ph.D. thesis, and some senior colleagues tried to get him fired from his instructorship. Their motives were a mixture of anti-Semitism, anti-Marxism, and, as he put it, their feeling that "I like to be stepped on" in both professional and married life. He astonished them by fighting back, forcing each in turn to admit his superior merits. He kept his job, and afterward steadily accumulated honors while his sense of estrangement increased.

"My successful explosion at Columbia"—as he called it in his journal—was so decisive that he never needed to repeat it. His colleagues, having thought he liked to be stepped on, did not make the same mistake twice. For the rest of his life he locked away his explosive feelings in his journals. He noticed that one result of the explosion was a new "sense of invulnerability...The feeling that I can now write with a new illumination, getting rid of that rigid linear method that has irritated me in my reviewing for so long...Effect visible in [Eugene] O'Neill essay." That essay seems to have been his first to use "we" in the disguised, contemptuous sense of "you but not I": "We demand that literature be a guide to life, and when we do that we put genius into a second place, for genius assures us of nothing but itself."

When his *Matthew Arnold* appeared in 1939, reviewers, apparently sensing its author's imperial ambitions, praised it not only with standard reviewers' hyperbole, but as a kind of national treasure. For Edmund Wilson, the book was "a credit both to his generation and to American criticism in general." In England, John Middleton Murray regretted only that "this particular glory should fall to the United States." The president of Columbia, Nicholas Murray Butler, read the reviews and used his statutory powers to grant Trilling tenure against the wishes of his English Department colleagues, and it was much remarked—by others—that he was the first tenured Jew in his department.

In his twenties, Trilling had been "deep in—and even contributed to—the literature of Jewish self-realization." In his thirties he felt alienated from Jewish culture, just as he later felt alienated from bourgeois, academic, and "adversary" cultures. In 1944 the *Contemporary Jewish Record* (the magazine of the American Jewish Committee before *Commentary*) surveyed young writers about their debt to their "Jewish heritage." Trilling answered:

I cannot discover anything in my professional intellectual life which I can specifically trace back to my Jewish birth and rearing. I do not think of myself as a "Jewish writer."

These sentences—often quoted by critics—sound as if he were making what one otherwise admiring critic complains was a "repudiation of Jewishness" simply because he didn't want to be a Jew. What he wrote a few paragraphs later, about the bad effects of Jewishness on those who embraced it, is rarely quoted but indicates the sharp edge of his motives. He had no qualms about being a Jew—he always said he enjoyed his Jewishness—but he was repelled by the ways in which he was being asked to think as a Jew and to submerge himself in what he saw as the narrow complacency of those Jews who, rather than fighting their way into American culture, chose a passive "adjustment" to their isolation from it, and took delusive, neurotic pride in having been chosen for exclusion:

> The literature of Jewish self-realization...attacked the sin of "escaping" the Jewish heritage; its effect...was to make easier the sin of "adjustment" on a wholly neurotic basis. It fostered a willingness to accept exclusion and even to intensify it,...to be provincial and parochial. It is in part accountable for the fact that the Jewish social group on its middle and wealthy levels... is now one of the most self-indulgent and self-admiring groups it is possible to imagine.

That group included the authors of the survey he was responding to.

In his journals Trilling thought about Jewishness in language he did not repeat in public. Shortly after World War II, he wrote at length about the ways in which nations and ethnic groups claim that their victimization by other groups exempts them from moral disapproval. "The modern technique for getting power—to claim that you *have none,* the more oppressed, the freer from responsibility." The Nazis came to power, he wrote, because the Germans could plausibly regard themselves as victims of the economic vengeance inflicted by the Versailles Treaty: "Germany had to conceive of itself as Jewish before it could make its demands—that is, as persecuted and discriminated against."

He only once found reason to think that Judaism might have anything more to it than a vague pride in bearing witness to the will of God even in the murderous injustices committed against Jews. In 1956 he read an article in *Commentary* about fifteenth-century Jews whose virtue, learning, and eloquence convinced many Russians, even in the Imperial Court, that Judaism was intellectually and spiritually superior to Eastern Orthodoxy. He wrote about it gratefully in his journals:

> I speak of the effect of this article, by which I mean the sense of satisfaction I felt in the idea, which seemed to me presented for the first time, that the Jews stood for something other than that vague and masochistic "testimony," that they represented a direct and conscious opposition to Christian belief.

Trilling regarded inherent Jewish identity as a mythical belief, and the fact that the Nazis committed mass murder partly because they thought the myth was true did not oblige him to believe it also.

III.

Trilling's calm, commanding presence in the lecture hall and his essays disguised the passion, anger, and pride that he released in his private journals. Among his colleagues in the Columbia English De-partment, he echoed Stephen Dedalus's words about his chosen exile:

> Who am I...to feel that these people are different in kind from me, and me superior? Yet feel it I do and must at this late age accept it....To accept it in secrecy and in absolute courtesy—it really needs silence and cunning, really needs the *mask*.

He exclaimed elsewhere: "What horror one is surrounded by!" His colleagues are at best "people of the intellect using the mind to sub-vert the reason," at worst "not people but palpitating self-protec-tions." Even at their best, they gave him

> the sense that these were not entire people, were simulacra of the way people are expected to be—and that this was the peculiar *Columbia* characteristic, this mild, virtuous two-dimensionality...

Venerated as a teacher, he records his "ever-growing dislike of teaching." Honored as the ideal image of his university, he is "wholly divorced from almost any aspect of it," yet unable to free himself: "there is no escape from the university for me." Talking with stu-dents and would-be disciples, "my mind was all rejection. Some filled me with horror." Those who study contemporary American litera-ture "dismay me....But then all graduate students trouble and in a way repel me." At intervals of a year or two, he convinced himself to accept a worshipful graduate student or untenured colleague as a disciple, then abruptly rejected him a few months later; sometimes it ended in tears. Trilling wrote a lament for the humanistic ideal, in which, he said, an educated person was an initiate who "became worthy of admission into the company of those who are thought to have transcended...mental darkness." More than one earnest critic of modern culture has endorsed this lament, apparently without noticing the irony in "are thought." Trilling wrote in his journals:

> I am *ashamed* of being in a university. I have one of the great reputations in the academic world. This thought makes me retch.

Trilling seems to have written his journals with a strong wish that they would someday be published—and an equally strong wish to keep some of them secret forever. Most great diarists, from Pepys through Byron to Virginia Woolf, never stopped to reflect or revise. Trilling wrote first drafts of his journal entries in pencil, on loose or spiral-bound pages that he called "notes," then selectively recopied them in ink in bound notebooks, improving the style, sometimes slightly bowdlerizing the content, but—as if he could not decide whether to conceal or reveal—he sometimes preserved both the pencil draft and the ink revision of the same entry. His journals portray himself as titanic both in pride and despair; even when he records "sexual difficulties" he attributes them to his mixed feelings about his public triumphs. He took great care to conceal from posterity anything that contradicted his titanic image of himself—but, in his characteristically divided way, recorded that act of concealment. He destroyed a year and a half of notes, he said, because they disgusted him when he reread them: "the *tone* of everything I wrote was so horrible—so touched with piousness, self-exculpation, accusation (often in the guise of 'forgiveness' or 'understanding')." He alluded to that destruction in his 1958 essay on *Lolita,* in an aside about anyone "who has tried to keep a journal and has been abashed at reading it by the apologetic, self-referring, self-exculpating whine of the prose, and by the very irony which is used to modify this deplorable tone."*

Trilling's secret disdain for his audience—a constant theme in his journals—is masked in his essays by his supremely self-confident, but also inviting, use of the first-person plural. In *The Liberal Imagination* the word "we" typically occurs three or four times on a page: "We who are liberal and progressive"; "the heaviness which we associate with 'reality'"; "We seem to like to condemn our finest but not our worst qualities"; "[Henry] James crowds probability rather closer than we nowadays like"; "We are inclined to flatter our own troubles with the belief that the nineteenth century was a peaceful time"; "We are likely not to want to agree with Hazlitt"; and hundreds more in the same style. What he meant by "we" was so famously elusive that he devoted the first page of *Beyond Culture* to other people's interpretations of his usage: "From time to time the essays I have published are reproached for making use of the pronoun 'we'," he began, "in a way that is said to be imprecise and indiscriminate." He neglected to explain that his statements of what "we believe" tended to be courtly euphemisms for "what you believe because you are visionless and conventional, and what I pretend to accept for civility's sake." His audience, he thought, could not bear to look directly at the abysses he described, so he framed his terrifying pictures in lulling rotundities.

W. H. Auden—who in the 1950s worked side by side with Trilling selecting and reviewing books for two influential upper-middlebrow book clubs, the Readers' Subscription and the Mid-Century Book

---

* Ironically enough, his public reputation as a sage still frustrates his evident wish for his journals to be published. More than one of his admirers has looked through them with the thought of printing them, but was too appalled by their contents to proceed.

Society—told friends that Trilling didn't like literature. Auden over-simplified, but he sensed something that Trilling also saw in himself. "It isn't that I don't like literature," he wrote in his journals, "it's that I don't like my relationship to literature.... I seem to be alienated from so many of the fine & complex figures of recent art and thought." He was alienated from many other figures. "The Victorians have lost all charm for me...They bore me utterly," he recorded. He also noted his "loathing of the subject of Am[erican] Lit[erature]." Meanwhile, in public, he was perfecting his venerable air of secular piety. He seemed to have learned, he said, "when I read a lecture, to impart a strong sense of an intellectual and moral occasion."

Trilling let himself be taken for a sober political thinker, though he sensed that readers tended to project their own politics on him, liberals finding an eloquent spokesmen for their ambivalent progressive views, conservatives finding encouragement in his doubts and worries about liberalism. One book about him is titled *Lionel Trilling: The Work of Liberation*; a very different one is titled *The Conservative Turn.** He was in fact far less interested in any political program than in the psychology that created it. "The liberal imagination" was his name for the sublimated worldview of a *bien-pensant* middle class that wanted no contact with imagination itself: "In the interests...of its vision of a general enlargement of freedom and rational direction in human life, [liberalism] drifts toward a denial of the emotions and the imagination." The unspoken and despairing implication is that we can have neither rationality nor freedom—ex-

---

* Trilling is often claimed as an intellectual father by American neoconservatives who imagine he was endorsing conservatism when he examined the contradictions that provoked liberalism to its ideas. In fact he thought liberalism had little to admire but that the alternatives were worse: "The conservative impulse and the reactionary impulse do not ...express themselves in ideas but only in action or in irritable mental gestures which seek to resemble ideas."

cept, as in Trilling's vision of *The Princess Casamassima,* when the two achieve perfect balance at the moment of death.

An idea, Trilling wrote, is "what comes into being when two contradictory emotions are made to confront each other." Liberalism, he thought, was a politics of ideas not action, and his phrase about emotions confronting each other seems to express admiration for the way liberalism taught itself to think about its own contradictions. Secretly, he thought a politics of ideas was bloodless and futile. Liberalism, he wrote in obscure and elliptical ways, repressed the frightening emotions that provoked its ideas, and left itself only with empty abstractions. He wrote in his journals that when someone begins "to court the liberal-democratic ideal, it is either a sign or the beginning of spiritual collapse in his work." Trilling saw his century as a long bleak history of the weakness of liberal politics of ideas against ideologies of force.

Trilling's reign ended in the theoretical revolutions of the 1960s. As rising academic stars began teaching literature in the language of structuralist and post-structuralist theory, and history as the product of impersonal, anonymous forces, Trilling's urbane meditations seemed merely fusty, his brief moments of ecstatic vision merely sentimental. The irony of Trilling's overthrow was that he secretly held the same views proclaimed by those who now dismissed him. He had hidden his nihilistic terrors and energies behind the urbane moralism of his style, and he had kept them secret, despite his recurring temptations to reveal them, in order to preserve the authority that he was now losing.

He never mentioned the "death of the author"—something the new theoretical criticism praised itself for discovering—but he had taught himself the same idea: that literature is produced by readers as much as by writers, and that the self is an illusion projected onto the world by an impersonal, indifferent, and inescapable culture. He wrote that "Tolstoi's reality" in *Anna Karenina* is the product of Tolstoy's "will and desire (and of ours)"—using a parenthesis to lower his voice while making a radical statement of the ways in which a book's meaning is shaped by the act of reading it.

As for the individual self, Trilling perceived it as so thoroughly ruled by impersonal exterior forces that he could imagine only one remaining escape "from the growing power of culture to control us by seduction or coercion"—and the escape he had in mind was nothing individual, personal, or voluntary, but the "stubborn core of biological urgency," the primal erotic impulse "that culture cannot reach." This, and this alone, "proposes to us that culture is not all-powerful." Trilling ignored, as too unlikely to bother with, any possibility that a private conscience or individual will could resist its surrounding culture. Unnoticed by everyone, he had invented the historical vision proclaimed by Michel Foucault, using the mild-sounding word "culture" to name what Foucault more strikingly called "power."

IV.

Trilling published a few short stories in the course of his life, but he finished and published only one novel, *The Middle of the Journey* (1947). It is written in a calm voice like that of an American E. M. Forster, with surprising interjections from D. H. Lawrence ("It was a soft destruction, almost voluptuous"). The book's memorably unsettling tension seems to be the effect of Trilling's ability to write secretly about one subject by pretending to write about another.

The book presents itself as a psychological study of 1930s politics, and every critic who wrote about it for sixty years treated it as a political novel, in the words of one, "an important document of the intellectual climate of the 1930s." Trilling himself taught that novels explore "the *actual*," their "field of...research being always the social world." His introduction to a 1975 reprint of *The Middle of the Journey* emphasizes the quest for social reality that produced the book:

> From my first conception of it, my story was committed to history—it was to draw out some of the moral and intellectual implications of the powerful attraction to Communism felt by a considerable part of the American intellectual class during the Thirties and Forties.

One character, Gifford Maxim, was "more consciously derived from actuality than any of the others": he was based on Whittaker Chambers. At the time Trilling wrote his novel, Chambers was not yet notorious for denouncing Alger Hiss as a Soviet spy during Hiss's years in Roosevelt's State Department. Trilling knew nothing about Hiss, but he had met Chambers in college and knew he had converted from a militant Communist operative to a militant Christian conservative who was now working as a well-known senior editor at *Time* magazine.

A few pages after explaining that Maxim was "consciously derived from actuality," Trilling changed his tone and wrote as if Maxim had not emerged from conscious actuality but had instead burst from Trilling's unconscious:

> Chambers had no part in my first conception and earliest drafts.... He came into the story fairly late in its development and wholly unbidden. Until he made his appearance I was not aware that there was any need for him, but when he suddenly turned up and proposed himself to my narrative, I could not fail to see how much to the point he was.

Maxim was so much to the point that he became the focus of the novel's secret inner plot, which, unlike the outer, visible plot, is not about politics but Eros.

The outer plot—the historical, political one—is realistic and edifying. John Laskell, recuperating from scarlet fever, makes a summer visit to his left-wing friends Arthur and Nancy Croom in a small Connecticut town. Earlier, in his New York sickroom, he had felt intense love for a rose, "a strange desire which *wanted* nothing...a love affair with non-existence...the removal of all the adverse conditions of the self." Just before he leaves for Connecticut, adverse conditions intrude themselves when Gifford Maxim returns from a long absence. He had disappeared into the Communist underground; now, having broken with the Party, he fears being murdered by his ex-comrades.

Three years before this, Laskell loved the gracious and beautiful Elizabeth Fuess, who died from pneumonia before they could marry. Maxim had been friendly with Elizabeth, and after her death, Laskell found "fortitude and comfort" in Maxim's "great, scarred, silent face." Now Maxim demands Laskell's help in making himself publicly visible and therefore less convenient to murder than if he stayed hidden.

The Crooms are appalled to hear that Maxim has betrayed their common cause, and Laskell gradually perceives the doctrinaire brutality concealed behind their earnest progressivism. Hostilities erupt when Maxim follows Laskell to Connecticut and the Crooms'. Maxim is aggressive and repulsive, but his guilt over the many murders committed by his Party has the effect of shattering Laskell's "moral certainty," his "little core of safety." Maxim, unlike the Crooms, knows that justice and mercy are real, not merely names attached to political actions. Maxim also knows that he and the

Crooms are allied despite their enmity: all three believe that truth is absolute and undivided, that it takes the form of some cohesive ideology. Laskell, who sees that truth is dialectical, that it cannot be fixed in a formula, rejects Maxim's deep certainties and the Crooms' shallow ones. In turn, Maxim and the Crooms feel toward Laskell "the anger of the masked will at the appearance of an idea in modulation."

At a tense Jamesian moment, Laskell tests Nancy Croom's morality and friendship by insisting to her that Maxim, through the friendship Maxim provided at the time of Elizabeth's death, now has an obscure "claim" on him. Nancy fails the test. She waves away the idea that Laskell's love for Elizabeth burdens him with an obligation to Maxim; she cannot even comprehend how he might think it. Nancy's husband also fails the test when he asks Laskell, "Aren't you being a little hypersubtle? A little too psychological?" Laskell knows the test was decisive:

Well, it had been done. The "claim" and Elizabeth's death had been brought together. They had been spoken in one sentence. Never before in his life had Laskell said anything to anybody in order to see if it would produce a particular response.

This is a crucial but unconvincing moment, because Laskell expects others to understand something that the novel itself doesn't make clear—how it is that Laskell, having once been in love with Elizabeth, is now irrevocably committed to Maxim. Laskell's obligation was clear to Trilling himself, however, because he knew that Elizabeth and Maxim were the same person. Elizabeth is an idealized portrait of the Diana whom Trilling courted, Maxim a nightmare image of the Diana to whom he was married. The uncomprehending

Crooms are the friends who cannot understand Trilling's loyalty to her, and his conviction that "Life is nothing unless sacrificial."*

Maxim erupts into Laskell's life with his phobias and aggressions, his black-and-white morality, his terror of solitude, his blunt insulting style, and his constant demand to be noticed and served. He begins his literary career by ordering Laskell to recommend him for a job with a left-wing monthly—as Trilling had started Diana's career by recommending her to *The Nation*. Trilling had fallen in love with Elizabeth Fuess and three years later found himself married to Gifford Maxim. He once wrote in a note to himself about novel-writing: "I think I can depend on the unconscious process working out a series of connecting and interesting incidents."

The secret plot of the novel is the story of the Trillings' honeymoon in 1929 in a Connecticut town exactly like the one where Laskell visits the Crooms. It reproduces the chronology of their summer there, portrays the townspeople they met, and, apparently, reports his listless ambivalence at the time. (During their honeymoon, Trilling wrote a story—published posthumously—about a man who, in the weeks before and after his marriage, is emotionally paralyzed by "a geyser of despair," a morbid jealousy over his wife's casual affairs before she met him.)

One episode in the novel seems to refer to events later than their honeymoon. Amid the anxieties provoked by Maxim's visit to Connecticut, Laskell finds brief, illicit satisfaction with an unsophisticated young married woman. Having loved "non-existence," Laskell, in one of his Lawrentian moments, perceives his young lover's "deep awareness of nullity, her knowledge of darkness." A reviewer dis-

---

* Trilling remained loyal to Gifford Maxim. In his introduction to a reprint of the novel, he called Whittaker Chambers "a man of honor." Diana Trilling was annoyed at his equanimity toward a right-wing ex-communist, but he was making a stoic affirmation of loyalty to both Chambers and Diana, despite public disapproval and his private reservations.

missed this episode as a "liberal middle-class dream of sex," but it evokes a real event that occurred early in Trilling's marriage, apparently an affair that Diana disguised in her memoir as the time "when Lionel began to lie to me and say that he was going to the library when, in fact, he was going to the movies." Her tone suggests that "the movies" was a euphemism. "I am unsure how I found this out," she says of Trilling's falsehood.

Trilling thought of artistic power and masculine sexual energy as two expressions of the same elemental, irrational force that he disdained and warned against in public. His novel hides its erotic agonies—Laskell's inescapable entanglement with Maxim's violence and energy—beneath its earnest, harmless liberalism. In his journals Trilling despaired over the social order that his criticism served: "How wonderful a conception is society in thought, how mean in actuality—death or surrender of passion and desire..." This was a more explicit statement of his sense that liberalism distrusted the emotions. He wrote after Ernest Hemingway died:

> Except Lawrence's thirty-two years ago, no writer's death has moved me as much—who would suppose how much he has haunted me? How much he existed in my mind—as a reproach? He was the only writer of our time I envied.

Hemingway, like the other "charismatic personalities" whom Trilling said he longed for, was a reproach because (as Trilling and almost everyone else imagined about Hemingway) he never compromised with civilization, never repressed his powers. Hemingway was often drunk and absurd, Trilling said in his journals, yet "How right such a man is compared to the 'good minds' of my university life." Trilling's experience confirmed his belief that his masculine powers could be released only by writing fiction. His only child was born nine months and twelve days after the publication date of his only novel.

V.

Trilling wrote in his book on E. M. Forster: "Surely if liberalism has a single desperate weakness it is an inadequacy of imagination: liberalism is always being surprised." This was the theme, spelled out in its preface, of *The Liberal Imagination*. That title sounded resonant and encouraging; no one else had yoked together liberalism and imagination in so compact and vivid a way. The fierce irony of the title—on a book that pointed to liberalism's fear of the imagination—went almost unnoticed. The book is still commonly described as a celebration of liberal values. Trilling had mixed feelings about his ironies, first concealing them in his soothing prose, then annoyed when no one noticed them. So many readers missed the ironies in *Beyond Culture* that he added a long note in a paperback reprint explaining them.

Trilling wrote much of *The Liberal Imagination* shortly before and shortly after he wrote *The Middle of the Journey,* and the creative energy that went into the novel spilled over the his essays. Rereading them a few years later, at a time when his work had diminished in subtlety and force, he wrote, "what genius I had then!" (In one of his many private echoes of the great, he was paraphrasing Swift looking back at *Gulliver.*) His essay "The Kinsey Report" suavely demolishes Kinsey's understanding of sex as a biological instinct: the report, Trilling wrote, never guesses that the gangster who goes to bed with a different woman every night may be driven by anxiety, not libido; it is unaware that one partner's satisfaction may depend on the other's; its survey of human-animal contacts "is, oddly, the only chapter

in the book which hints that sex may be touched with tenderness."
(Trilling's wit was infrequent but sharp. Lillian Hellman, he wrote in
his journals, was "a greatly underdepreciated woman.")

"Freud and Literature," also in *The Liberal Imagination,* demon-
strates with examples that psychoanalytic insight can illuminate literature without distorting it. Trilling's journals suggest that a few
years after writing this essay, his own long psychoanalysis began to
illuminate him to himself, and his later essays treat Freud in a darker
way as the prophet of a bleak religion of self-knowledge without
hope. The Freud of Trilling's later years had not only "made it apparent . . . how entirely implicated in culture we all are," but also, through
a deep paradox of the self, had shown that only the drive toward
death, the *Todestrieb,* can lead to a "self beyond the reach of culture." *Beyond Culture* was another ironic title. In the 1930s Trilling
had been tempted by a Communist faith that would have obliged him
to take political action. He chose instead a Freudian faith that, in his
heterodox version of it, regarded all action as neurotic and futile. He
revered an imaginary Freud, created in his own image, who found
hope only in "biological urgency." He now ignored the real Freud
who had a different view, who had written that "the voice of the intellect is a soft one, but it does not rest till it has gained a hearing,"
and who heard in that conscious intellectual voice "one of the few
points on which one may be optimistic about the future of mankind."

Trilling's notes on his psychoanalytic treatment are concerned
mostly with his "sexual difficulties," which had begun "at the point
of my beginning to be successful, i.e. with the publication of
M[atthew] A[rnold]." Success as an academic critic—success that required opposition to his deepest, most creative self—had discouraged
his sexuality, just as his success at publishing a novel had briefly encouraged it. The public triumph of *The Liberal Imagination* in 1950
seems to have worsened his difficulties more or less permanently.

Over the next few years, reviewers wondered aloud at the darker mood of the essays he wrote after 1950 and collected in *The Opposing Self* (1955) and *A Gathering of Fugitives* (1956). A decade's further essays in *Beyond Culture* prompted George Steiner to mourn the loss of a style that "had been in the 1940s a toughly argued subtlety" but was now "a somewhat saddened academic preciousness."

Diana Trilling ends her memoir of their marriage in 1950, leaving their later years in silence. It was her decision, however, to give her husband's journals to the Columbia University Library, knowing that she was giving access to his own account of the marriage. Those journals make clear that from 1950 onward, the "resentment so central to our marriage" went both ways, and he indicates, without being explicit, that he now felt obliged to ease Diana's resentment by providing for her what he himself could no longer provide, by encouraging one of his disciples toward—and perhaps into—her bed. Around this time, he notes his "growing interest in the idea of orgy," another way of dissolving his private relation to her. With Diana's ambivalent complaisance, he now fell in love with the young wife of a middle-aged political journalist who had left his job to study for a graduate degree at Columbia. The young woman reciprocated his feelings: "Nothing in my life is of importance except you," he records her telling him. (The woman's husband, with Trilling's complaisance, took an interest in Diana, who seems to have reciprocated it until she was repelled by his coarse sexual talk about his wife.)

Trilling wrote two versions of a lengthy journal entry—one written in a pencil on a loose sheet, the other written in ink in a bound notebook—describing a party given by the journalist and his wife. In the draft version, the young woman kisses Trilling in the kitchen in front of the servants; in the notebook version she merely touches him. (Having airbrushed the story for the second version he characteristically chose also to preserve the first). Outside the kitchen, Trilling,

Diana, and Trilling's disciple—the three arrived and left together—kept up appearances by projecting Olympian distaste: "Oh to be proconsular and responsible!" Trilling exclaimed in bitter irony, recalling "our grave dignified remoteness" in the midst of the secret indignities of his life.

Almost all of Trilling's journal entries about his relation with the young woman seem to have been lost when he discarded a year and a half of notes in disgust over their self-pity. The note in which he records that act of destruction refers to the whole episode as "the Great Instauration and its collapse." *The Great Instauration* was the title of Francis Bacon's 1620 project to restore the world to its original state of paradise, and was Trilling's name for his project to restore both his erotic and literary powers. In her memoir, written almost forty years later, Diana Trilling alluded vaguely to this episode, sympathizing, whatever the cost to her marriage, with his hopes for recovery: "I could have wished him to have a thousand mistresses were this to have released him from the constraints upon him as a writer of fiction." At the time, she was far less happy about his methodical, experimental efforts at instauration. He noted in his journal: "D's anger at my 'betrayal' of our past—'For you it's research.' The next morning she speaks bitterly of my 'depersonalization' of her, of myself."

Trilling's journals give no details of "the Great Instauration and its collapse," but he seems to have left an elliptical public record in his essay on *Lolita,* an essay that became famous because Trilling—the great public exponent of rectitude—praised the scandalous book as a story "not about sex, but about love." His review culminated in an exalted hymn to the kind of unconsummated courtly love that "could not possibly exist in marriage," a hymn even to the kind of unrequited love that could issue only in a "passion so unrewarding, so humiliating." (What is odd about this is that Humbert Humbert's passion, however humiliating, was consummated night after night; the essay is a variation on Trilling's earlier vision of a love that desires nothing in *The Princess Casamassima*.) The aftermath of the episode was the quietist mood of his later years—"my lack of all hope, of all desire for hope," as he wrote in his journal—a mood that later critics mistook for conservatism. When he wrote that the only hope for escape from culture was the "stubborn core of biological urgency," he was writing about a hope that he had now lost.*

Far from raging against his diminished hopes, Trilling was relieved to expect less of himself. He had now settled himself, he wrote with his usual irony, "in a happy equality" with his disciple's lesser intellect. He was grateful for the relationship between them: "how it has diminished my sense of myself, very pleasurably to be sure, how it has led me to think of myself as being quieter and with less force, how it has lessened tension, in myself and in relation to D[iana]." A few years later, he contrasted his quietude with the egoistic madness of Saul Bellow and Norman Mailer: "To impose, to impose: this is their single aim; it acts as a real thing, although it rises out of the absurdity" of their belief in their own myths. "I defeated myself long ago when I rejected the way of chutzpah and mishagass in favor of reason and diffidence."

In public and in the classroom he maintained his courtly mask of sober authority. The mask slipped only once, in a late essay in which he lampooned the undergraduate students who were awed by his authority. Their minds moved, he wrote, "through the terrors and mysteries of modern literature like so many Parsifals, asking no questions at the behest of wonder and fear." He was accustomed himself to the

---

* American neo-conservatism, with its insistent worry over individual and national "manliness," is transparently the product of sexual anxieties as well as political ones, and found its philosophical origins in the essays that issued from Trilling's erotic despair.

idea that human beings were expressions of their culture, that, except in the rare case of a Lawrence or Hemingway, he scarcely imagined them existing as persons at all—so he had no hesitation in writing about his students as a collective culture, whatever dismay they might feel in reading what he thought about them.

He had never liked his "connection to literature," and a few years before his death he seems to have lost interest in it, even as he continued to fulfill his obligations as a sage by writing about it. In his journal he treated his unhappiness as the product of his own sad heroism, as if he had actively sundered himself from literature, rather than merely growing bored by it: "My having broken my connection with literature. In favor of what? Alas."

His last book, *Sincerity and Authenticity* (1972), was a battlefield report from the conflict between his private and public selves, in the form of a history of the "moral idioms" that art deploys to conceal or reveal personality. He ended the book by contrasting the daemonic madness of someone who fantasizes he is Christ—a madness praised by the psychiatrist David Cooper as a doorway to truth—with the responsible sanity of the real Christ, who accepted

> the inconveniences of undertaking to intercede, of being a sacrifice, of reasoning with rabbis, of making sermons, of having disciples, of going to weddings and funerals, of beginning something and at a certain point remarking that it is finished.

Trilling, as he saw it, had accepted all these "inconveniences," interceding in campus disputes, sacrificing himself to his wife and (in her words) "to decency," reasoning with professors, making lectures, training academic disciples, attending public functions. The last words of his book were Christ's last words from the cross: "It is finished." Trilling had at last united his warring "Olympian" and "sacrificial" impulses in a single straight-faced claim that his life and career had been Christlike.

A few chapters earlier he had mentioned "the peculiar bitterness of modern man, the knowledge that he is not a genius." Trilling's private bitterness was the knowledge that he had made a sacrifice of his genius by suppressing it—"In favor of what?" In his characterization of modern man, as in all his generalizations about what "we" know and believe, he made a silent, tentative exception for himself.

2

MORALIST: DWIGHT MACDONALD

I.

IN HIS LONG career as a journalist and critic, Dwight Macdonald exasperated his left-wing friends by changing his political views unpredictably and abruptly, sometimes between soup and dessert. He signed a petition favoring one side in a labor dispute, only to join the other side a few days later. He was a Trotskyite; then he was a pacifist; later he was neither. He wrote to a friend: "My own political views for years ... have been tentative, contradictory, and deplorably vague."

His elitist views on literature and art seemed to undercut his populist politics. He despised almost everything in popular culture; some best-selling books are remembered today only because of the delighted exuberance with which he demolished them in a review. At sixty-two, when he joined the protesters at the 1968 campus uprising at Columbia, he lectured to the student rebels on the value of critical standards and high culture. Even his sympathetic biographer, Michael Wreszin, used the title of his 1994 biography—*A Rebel in Defense of Tradition*—to point toward Macdonald's contradictions and emphasized his "split personality, the agitating activist vs. the incisive cultural critic."

Memorial tributes to him tended to condescend to his ideas while praising the refined clowning of his style: "the most important thing" Macdonald left behind, one critic writes, was "a singular, wised-up, cant-free voice that is pure intelligence at play." The comments on the cover of a recent selection of his work praise him mostly as a contrarian, provoker, and scourge of mediocrity, memorable not for what he said about closed political debates or forgotten writers, but for having had, as Norman Mailer put it, "the rare gift of always speaking out of his own voice."

Macdonald was a deeper, more decisive, and far more coherent thinker than his reputation suggests. He was consistent in his focus on the moral aspects of books and politics, but the literary essays that made him famous tended to treat such matters either in passing or in a tone of embarrassment. He gestured toward them in a memorial essay on James Agee in 1957:

> Agee, I think, had the technical, the intellectual, and the moral equipment to do major writing. By "moral," which has a terribly old-fashioned ring, I mean that Agee believed in and—what is rarer—was interested in good and evil. Lots of writers are fascinated by evil and write copiously about it, but they are bored by virtue.... (Character is another old-fashioned quality that interested Agee.)

Macdonald's greatest achievement was his magazine *Politics* (1944–1949), which had a small circulation and a large impact. Czesław Miłosz later told him that his magazine had had a far greater effect in Europe than he could have guessed from America.*

---

* Miłosz wrote an essay in praise of Macdonald, "a specific American type—the completely free man, capable of making decisions at all times about all things strictly according to his personal moral judgment."

A typical issue might include Albert Camus's refusal to choose between evil alternatives, "Neither Victims nor Executioners," or Bruno Bettelheim's report from the Nazi concentration camps, "Behavior in Extreme Situations"—the first such account to appear—or Simone Weil's "The Iliad, or The Poem of Force," which transformed the modern view of Homer while illuminating both ancient literature and contemporary morality. The same double focus on aesthetics and morality later became Macdonald's greatest strength as a critic.

Politics differed from all other political magazines by treating politics as a branch of morals. Near the end of its run, Macdonald compiled a "Subject Index" to its back numbers; the first entry was "Political Morality." He asked the same questions about political values that he asked about aesthetic ones. His magazine was both an urgent commentary on current events and a patient meditation on the deeper ways those events should be judged. In a typical issue the front pages condemned Roosevelt's indifference to Jewish refugees, and the back pages analyzed the limits of Marxist ethics as a way of interpreting history.

The same monthly issue that reported on French elections and strikes by conscientious objectors also printed an essay in which Macdonald explored basic questions about the values he relied on in both his political critiques and his aesthetic ones:

By "value judgment" I mean a statement that involves the notion of "Good" and "Bad" in either an ethical or an esthetic sense.... The "personal feeling" of the observer not only enters into the judgment but is the chief determinant of the judgment. It is impossible, therefore, ever to solve a moral or esthetic problem in the definite way that a scientific problem can be solved....

A few years later he wrote, "I think that the only serious aspect of politics is its relation to art and morality."

Macdonald's essays on literature and culture display his genius for what he called "the genres that one would expect our age to excel in,...rhetoric and comedy." "Masscult and Midcult," published in 1960, takes gleeful pleasure in deflating *The Old Man and the Sea* and other earnest, high-sounding books and plays that served an audience who aspired to be intellectual and avant-garde without being either. Unlike mass-produced popular culture, "midcult"—Macdonald's Soviet-sounding shorthand for middlebrow culture—"pretends to respect the standards of High Culture while in fact it waters them down and vulgarizes them." Thornton Wilder's *Our Town* is an example:

> The stage manager is its demiurge. He is the perfect American pragmatist, folksy and relaxed because that's jest the way things are and if anybuddy hankers to change 'em that's their right only (pause, business of drawing reflectively on pipe) chances are 't won't make a sight of difference (pipe business again) things don't change much in Grover's Corners. There is no issue too trivial for him not to take a stand on. "That's the end of the first act, friends," he tells the audience. "You can go smoke now"—adding with a touch of genius, "those that smoke." Don't do any harm, really, one way or t'other.

Readers who come to this without knowing Macdonald's less exuberant political essays can easily miss his moral point while smiling over his aesthetic one. *Our Town* is not merely artistically defective; it is morally defective. Grover's Corners can't be changed by anyone's choices; no one's judgment matters, one way or t'other; the height of wisdom is to accept "the way things are." At the heart of Macdonald's career as a political journalist was his hatred of passive acceptance, his contempt for any argument that the "lesser evil" should be endured in order to evade the greater one.

By tolerating, among much else, the "lesser evil" of Stalinism in the war against the greater evil of Nazism, the Allies had assured "the triumph of the greater evil in a different form." At the start of the cold war, "the world, having avoided being hanged by Hitler, is being poisoned by the victors." Once, in the middle of a sentence about the "lesser evil," he interrupted himself with a dash followed by an exclamation: "—the pages and pages of argumentation I have written exposing the illogic and immorality of this position!"

Near the end of "Masscult and Midcult" Macdonald quotes a long passage from Kierkegaard's *The Present Age* about what happens when a person becomes a member of that empty phantom, "the public." He follows the quotation with a single closing sentence: "This is the essence of what I have tried to say." In other words, Macdonald was writing less about bad art and greedy publishers than about what it means to let oneself disappear into a passive and anonymous public. Reviewers complained that Macdonald didn't like the masses. What he didn't like was anyone's willingness to be submerged into a mass and the culture that profited each time someone sank into it.

Macdonald's essays are pervaded by his moral sensibility, even when he seems to be writing only about aesthetics. In the famous review in which he marches through James Gould Cozzens's midcult novel *By Love Possessed,* devastating not only the book but also the rapturous reception it got from almost everyone else, he seems to take offense only at Cozzens's intellectual and aesthetic failures—until the final paragraphs, where he unobtrusively changes the subject. At the end of Tolstoy's *The Death of Ivan Ilyich,* he writes, Ilyich "feels free because he is compelled to reject his past as 'not the right thing'"; he has made a morally decisive choice. At the end of

By Love Possessed, Cozzens's hero Arthur Winner, "for complicated pragmatic-sentimental reasons,...is allowed to accept his past, is even thanked by his best friend for having concealed from him the fact that he had cuckolded him." The passive acceptance that the novel portrays and performs is the same moral failure that Macdonald saw in *Our Town:*

> The last words of the book are Winner's...: "I'm here." It's all right, nothing has to be changed: "I have the strength, the strength to, to—to endure more miseries," thinks Winner, gratefully.

Midcult critics, like Stalinist ones, "assumed it was good for writers to identify themselves with their society, which in turn assumed the society was good." Macdonald valued the modernist avant-garde of Joyce, Eliot, Picasso, and Stravinsky not for the aesthetic and coterie reasons favored by his friends, but because, in his eyes, it had made a moral judgment by refusing to accept its society as good.

II.

Macdonald often evokes literary "standards" in that way that suggests he was a reactionary defender of eternal truths. He makes it clear, though less often, that he was not. From his essay "The Triumph of Fact":

> An umpire, like a scientist, deals with measurable phenomena according to generally accepted rules, but the critic works with standards peculiar to himself, although they somehow corre-

spond to standards each of his readers has individually developed....While Faulkner's superiority over Marquand cannot be proved, it can be demonstrated. This is a different operation involving an appeal—by reason, analysis, illustration, and rhetoric—to cultural values which critic and reader have in common, values no more susceptible of scientific statement than are the moral values-in-common to which Jesus appealed but which, for all that, exist as vividly and definitely as do mercy, humility, and love.

Politics, like aesthetics, was ultimately a matter of personal morality, not the expression of impersonal historical forces. Against the fantasy that mass movements could set a common agenda for individual persons, he wrote: "Socialism is primarily an ethical matter. The number of people who want it at any given moment has nothing to do with its validity for the individual who makes it his value." Because Macdonald saw politics as a means of putting moral values into practice, he felt obliged to change his political views—abandoning his pacifism, accepting a lesser-evil argument in the face of postwar Stalinism—when he saw that they had diverged from his ethical ones.

He never expected politics and ethics to coincide exactly. He wrote to a friend:

You are right about the necessity of redefining Justice and other values in the light of concrete historical conditions, but there must also be an absolute, nonhistorically relative content to be redefined.... More and more I come up against the fact that we must face and live with contradictions of this kind (Justice is both historically relative, as Marx said it was, and absolute, as Plato did), must live dangerously intellectually...

Sectarians on the left believed justice to be relative; on the right, absolute. Both views, Macdonald thought, led to injustice; both were tempting because they offered a straightforward solution to an impossible problem. Relative and absolute justice could never be reconciled, and Macdonald believed that real injustice could be resisted only by those who understood this, who refused the safety of sectarian dogma and chose instead to "live dangerously intellectually." Gandhi—"the last political leader in the world who was a person, not a mask or a radio voice or an institution"—triumphed partly because he was unbothered by the contradiction between his absolute ideals and his "compromised" politics.

Macdonald believed that an active subjective judgment was a more valid way to approach moral reality than any fixed, established system, whether it based itself on allegedly scientific Marxist authority or on divine authority. And he believed that subjective judgment was required in order to achieve any real community:

> I think each man's values come from intuitions which are peculiar to himself and yet—if he is talented as a moralist—also strike common chords that vibrate respondingly in other people's consciences. This is what ethical teachers have always done; it is the only way we have learned anything essential about ethics or communicated our discoveries to others....

He took it for granted that even if morality could only be approached subjectively, it was still, as Wittgenstein said about ethics, "a condition of the world, like logic," not a set of rules, not merely a way of thinking. A moral course of action was therefore always a pragmatic one, even when appearances argued otherwise. A typical headline in *Politics* asked the question "How 'Practical' Is a Racially Segregated Army?," which Macdonald answered by demonstrating on both practical and moral grounds that common-sense arguments for segregation were "uncommon nonsense." The Allies' "appalling 'unconditional surrender' policy" in World War II, he wrote in 1945, was both immoral and impractical. It convinced the German people, "as Hitler's most frenetic orations could not have convinced them, that their only hope was to stand firm behind the Nazis"; it refused support to the July 1944 conspirators who hoped to assassinate Hitler and negotiate peace; it prolonged the war at the cost of thousands of lives. "Illogic and immorality," as he called them, were inseparable from each other. Hardheaded realists who could not recognize their moral failures could never understand their practical ones.

What produced the characteristic disasters of twentieth-century politics was the exclusion of subjective, personal thinking from political programs—not merely its obvious exclusion from totalitarian politics, but also from the principled political thinking of many pacifists and others with equally admirable attitudes. As always in Macdonald, an aesthetic deficiency—such people were "somewhat boring...a little on the dull side"—was a sign of ethical deficiency:

Intellectually, their ideas lack subtlety and logical structure. Ethically, they are *too* consistent; they don't sense the tragedy of life, the incredible difficulty of actually putting into practice an ethical concept. They have not succumbed to temptation because they have never been tempted; they are good simply because it has never occurred to them to be bad. They are, in a word, unworldly.

A moral point of view, in the absence of a complex and contradictory personality, was merely theoretical, impractical, futile.

Gandhi, in contrast, was "not at all unworldly," and he could be as effective as he was because he never suppressed his personality in the way that his popular image suggested; he was "full of humor, slyness, perversity, and—above all—practicality." Even his asceticism, his revulsion against gluttony, luxury, and sexual indulgence, was a sign of his worldliness, his sense of how serious and inescapable was his and others' "deep drive... *toward* gluttony, luxury, and sexual indulgence."

Almost everything Macdonald wrote, including his comic parodies and his rhetorical set-pieces, seems to have been written in the voice of his private conscience. When he reprinted his essays he typically peppered them with such renunciatory footnotes as, "Untrue, indeed the reverse of the truth," or, "No! No! Marxistical baby-talk!"* Hannah Arendt, noting his reputation for "changing his mind," observed:

> No one, of course, who is willing to listen to reason and to reality can help changing his mind, but most of us do this imperceptibly, hardly being aware of our changes, whereas Macdonald in a veritable furor of intellectual integrity and moral honesty sets out to hunt down his "mistakes," without ever changing the record in the slightest, his technique being to annotate his earlier articles with refutations of himself.

Czesław Miłosz wrote of Macdonald's self-refutations: "that freedom, that breath of man in the lines of print, is invigorating." If his commentaries on himself could have been read in Communist-era

---

* He began his attacks on his earlier work in 1953 when he reprinted two essays from the 1940s in a pamphlet, *The Root is Man*. He continued the practice, adding footnotes and afterwords in his later collections of political and literary essays: *The Responsibility of Peoples* (1957, published at the time only in the UK), *Memoirs of a Revolutionist* (1960, republished in 1970 as *Politics Past*), *Against the American Grain* (1962), and *Discriminations* (1974).

Poland, "by their contrast with the obligatory style over there they would have said a great deal about the essence of unfreedom, which is most horrifying when it enters the blood, when it appears *normal*." Macdonald heeded his conscience even when it made painful accusations, and he seems to have been untempted by the all too common tendency among the conscience-stricken to denounce someone else instead for faults that one can't bear to acknowledge in oneself. The only thing that silenced him when his rhetoric was in flood was his conscience; his friends noticed they could always shut him up in an argument by accusing him of unconscious anti-Semitism. Long after his death, he still provoked, in some reviewers, name-calling fury so intense that it suggests that his essays give unwelcome voice to a reader's conscience as well as to his own.

III.

Dwight Macdonald was born in 1906 and christened with the family name of his father's grandmother. The Dwight family of New England was to Yale what the Adams, Eliot, and Lowell families were to Harvard. Each family produced one or more soberly respectable presidents of the college or the nation. Each produced a volatile and often tormented moralist-aesthete: Henry Adams, T. S. Eliot, Robert Lowell, Dwight Macdonald.

At Yale, Macdonald had no politics but was already brash about his aesthetics. When the college newspaper refused to print his column accusing an English professor of incompetence, he tried to circulate it as a handbill. Threatened with expulsion, he suppressed the piece. In later life his offended conscience forbade such compromises—and he denounced himself afterward when he disobeyed it.

He graduated in 1928, convinced that the future belonged to

America's businessmen, not to its artists and writers. A few months' training for an executive post at Macy's convinced him otherwise. He found a job with Henry Luce's sumptuous new business magazine *Fortune*; he disliked the subject matter but liked the paycheck, and his energetic style made prosaic corporations sound exciting even when he criticized them. His contempt for business was apolitical until the Great Depression impelled him to find a social conscience. He married Nancy Rodman, an heiress with Communist leanings who encouraged his emerging Marxism. (Her brother Selden Rodman edited the left-wing monthly *Common Sense*.) In 1936 Macdonald quit *Fortune* after provoking his editors with a Marxist analysis of the steel industry and refusing to accept their red-penciling.

By 1937, appalled by Stalinism, he was a committed Trotskyite. The future that he had once thought belonged to businessmen, he was now convinced belonged to the working class. In *Partisan Review* and other more-or-less Trotskyite magazines he welcomed the impending socialist revolution and pitied *The New Yorker* (still displaying the sophisticated lightness it began with in the 1920s) as "an accurate expression of a decaying social order"—to which he himself contributed by printing a few pieces there in the 1930s. By the early 1940s, events had refuted all his predictions, notably his expectations of a "Third Front" that would rise up against both sides in World War II, and he abandoned his fantasies of any inevitable future. The future belonged to no one. It would be made, he now insisted, not by destiny or any immutable force but by conflicts among free individual choices—including ones made by evil dictators and those who resisted them.

Macdonald's failure as a prophet freed him to be critical, ironic, and hortatory with no illusion that he spoke on behalf of the future or as a mouthpiece for infallible doctrine. Responding to a letter complaining that *Politics* was a "treacherous and obstructive" magazine, he defended himself by quoting one of his intellectual heroes writing about another, Alexander Herzen on Proudhon: "His strength lay not in construction but in criticism." "The motto on his shield," Macdonald later wrote of himself, "is a bold '*YES BUT—*.'"

In his essays for *Partisan Review* he had tended to write as a collective "we." Now he wrote in the first-person singular. *Politics* was a one-man magazine that expressed his own views—but also those of Georges Bataille, Simone de Beauvoir, Paul Goodman, Marshall McLuhan, George Orwell, and angry readers and friends who disputed everything he wrote. He observed that his one-man magazine presented a wider variety of opinion than could be found in committee-run magazines like *Partisan Review.*

Macdonald kept *Politics* focused on what he called in a letter "the great theme of our day...moral responsibility and courage." His magnificent 1945 essay "The Responsibility of Peoples" detailed the logical and moral faults of arguments that accused the German people of collective guilt for the death camps—or the American and British people for the mass bombing of civilians. Collective guilt was real, Macdonald added, but only when an entire community approved or participated in the crime—as in lynchings in the American South. Many years later he found evidence of collective guilt in American opinion polls that favored the bombing of Vietnam.

His essays in *Politics* annoyed or outraged many of his friends, but, he recalled later, "it was, oddly enough, the emphasis on morality that caused the most scandal." Irving Howe, in a response to Macdonald titled "The 13th Disciple," shuddered over "the dangerous waters in which he is wading," dangerous because "from talk of Absolute Morality to talk of God...is but a short step." Howe needn't have worried. As Macdonald wrote later, "Religion...bores me even more than Marxism"; both, in his view, falsely offered impersonal truths that were independent of personal convictions; the only truths that mattered to persons—in other words, that weren't boring—were the ones that could be approached or attained through personal conviction.

Bored as he was by Marxism, he retained some Marxist ways of thinking. His analysis of mass culture depended heavily on the idea of an economic base concealed by a cultural superstructure; both masscult and midcult produced commodity art on an industrial scale; both were celebrity cultures that circulated another "commodity, Personality." Like Engels on Balzac, Macdonald valued works of art that, against their maker's intention, revealed truths about the society they intended to celebrate: Leni Riefenstahl's *Triumph of the Will* is "evilly motivated,...but since she is an artist she can't help clarifying" what Nazism really was. Although Macdonald "never had any interest in religion, or God," he always had "much in Jesus, none in Christ"—the moral man, not the anointed savior. From his New England Congregationalist ancestors to Macdonald the "good Christian atheist," as he once described himself, was but a short step. Macdonald worked toward an absolute secular morality at the same time, and in much the same spirit, that Dietrich Bonhoeffer, in a Nazi prison cell, was working toward a "religionless Christianity."

Macdonald's pacifism led him to oppose American participation in the war against Germany, and in 1947 he wrote an essay that gave moral and practical answers to the question "Why Destroy Draft Cards?" But by 1948 he confronted what he called "the pacifist dilemma": there was no pacifist answer to the Soviet blockade of Berlin, just as there had been no pacifist answer (he now acknowledged) to Chamberlain's capitulation at Munich ten years earlier. Macdonald began to doubt "the political validity of a 'Utopian'...position," and renounced pacifism soon afterward.

His views on private life had changed in parallel with his political ones. He and his wife had both grown dissatisfied with their companionable marriage; she began having affairs; he followed her example. Unexpectedly, one of his affairs lasted for years and he kept hoping it would lead to marriage. He found, he said, "a relationship unique in my life, a spontaneous, equal, reciprocal ... relation with a woman, which began on a sexual plane and developed into the strongest emotional tie I have ever felt." He told a friend: "reason, skepticism, irony, satire—these were my qualities until ... somewhere around the middle of editing *Politics*, I began more and more to feel the importance of Love." At "the absurd age of 40," he said, he developed "for the first time a real interest in women." His second marriage, some years later, to Gloria Lanier, was affectionate, stormy, and passionate.

Through his two sons by his first wife he discovered a "deep feeling" for children, though mostly for those with whom he could talk as he talked with adults. During his summers on Cape Cod he often gathered a crowd of his neighbors' children and his own for an afternoon of games and movies. His older son never forgave one of his other Cape Cod habits, the nude cocktail parties he hosted on the beach for the summering intellectuals.

In the 1950s Macdonald mostly lost interest in politics because, he said, it offered no moral problems worth thinking about. It took little effort to understand Stalinism as a great evil, more dangerous even than Nazism because it won support by claiming moral purpose. The evils of American mass culture were less obvious but still urgent:

If the US doesn't or cannot change its mass culture ... it will lose the war against [the] USSR. Americans have been made into permanent adolescents by advertising, mass culture—uncritical, herdminded, pleasure-loving, concerned about trivia of materialistic living, scared of death, sex, old age....

Macdonald took a job as a staff writer at *The New Yorker* in 1952 and used its glossy, prosperous pages as a medium for his social conscience. In his first months there he wrote a two-part profile of Dorothy Day, a sustained portrait of courage, self-denial, and eccentricity, with only a few of the comic touches required by the magazine's style. In 1963, his long impassioned *New Yorker* essay on Michael Harrington's *The Other America* passed from hand to hand in the White House and prompted John F. Kennedy to launch his anti-poverty program. For *Partisan Review*, now subdued from its Trotskyite beginnings, he wrote a fighting defense of Hannah Arendt's *Eichmann in Jerusalem* in the midst of the Kulturkampf against it; she had been accused of slandering the victims with her unflattering account of Jewish leaders in the wartime ghettos—but the campaign against her was driven, Macdonald insisted, by ethnic loyalties indifferent to morality and truth.*

Around the same time, in monthly film reviews in *Esquire* he demonstrated to its masculine audience that aesthetic pleasure can coexist with moral intelligence. *Esquire* also gave him a platform where he could again write about politics, but now in a style of extravagant fantasy, making moral arguments without feeling any obligation to concern himself with practicalities. One of his *Esquire* essays proposed wholesale amendments to the Constitution, eliminating the presidency, establishing city-states, and requiring spending on poverty to keep pace with spending on space exploration.

The Vietnam War brought him back to the podium and the barricades. During the Columbia *événements* of 1968, he lost friends when he publicized his support for Students for a Democratic Soci-

---

*A dozen years earlier, Macdonald had praised her argument in *The Origins of Totalitarianism* that the "bourgeois family man" could be the agent and embodiment of totalitarian oppression. This argument outraged no one until, in *Eichmann in Jerusalem*, she applied it to bourgeois family men who were also victims of totalitarianism.

ety—support that was clear-eyed and often critical, and which he withdrew as SDS turned violent. He argued in letters to friends and newspapers that a moral protest against injustice will always attract amoral thugs who give the authorities an excuse to discredit it, but he refused to be distracted from the moral urgency of the protest itself.

Macdonald died in 1982, dispirited by years of ill health when he drank too much and wrote too little. In his almost silent years before his death he had already begun to remembered mostly for his extravagant style and his Quixotic enthusiasms. Many of his admirers, embarrassed by the "terribly old-fashioned ring" of his ideas about the permanent truths of justice and injustice, by his sense that aesthetics were inseparable from morality, and slightly wearied by his rebukes, preferred to imagine him as a great entertainer, not as he was, the most entertaining of the great prophets.

3

OUTSIDER: ALFRED KAZIN

I.

IN BOTH HIS life and his writings Alfred Kazin was divided between two ideas of what it meant to be a Jew in America, one that he was committed to, and one that tempted him.

He was committed to the idea that a Jew was an outsider, with no special loyalties to a collective identity, not even that of other Jews, and that a Jew could therefore sympathize with other outsiders, regardless of their ethnicity, skin color, or other marker of identity. To be a Jew was, for him, to be an individual, with all of individuality's responsibility, loneliness, and willingness to take risks, someone whose deepest concern was justice—justice for all other outsiders as well as for himself. Whenever Kazin lapsed from this commitment, he later returned to it with a sense of exhilaration at seeing clearly again.

Yet he was repeatedly tempted by the idea that a Jew was a member of a separate and unique group of people, loyal to one another and their history, with a collective experience that differed from all others. To be a Jew, in this way of thinking, was to share in a group identity to which individuality must ultimately be sacrificed, and to be concerned most deeply with power—power wielded by other groups against one's own, and power that one's own group can gain through alliances with those more powerful. Kazin slipped into this temptation whenever he despaired about politics or himself.

Kazin was a literary critic and a memoirist whose best books were *On Native Grounds* (1942), the first of seven volumes of criticism, each mostly or entirely about American literature, and *A Walker in the City* (1951), the first of three volumes of memoirs. He wrote hundreds of lectures, essays, and reviews on books, culture, and politics, and kept a journal almost every day of his adult life. He published some sanitized and rewritten excerpts from his journal in a late book, *A Lifetime Burning in Every Moment* (1996); excerpts from the raw originals were published after his death. He taught for a semester or two at each of a dozen different colleges, then had two tenured professorships. He spent much of his time on the road, giving public lectures and attending boring conferences.

The young Jack Kerouac, after an hour in Kazin's classroom, wrote, "I like this guy because he is excited." Kazin suspected some of his intellectual rivals of using literature as a ladder for social climbing; his own excitement went deeper. His third wife, Ann Birstein, in her memoir *What I Saw at the Fair* (2003), reports that he was sexually aroused by intense literary discussion. His excitement over his life, as recorded in his journal—and in Richard M. Cook's *Alfred Kazin: A Biography* (2008)—was alternately infectious and appalling: infectious when Kazin fights the good fight against hypocrisy, bootlicking, and complacency; appalling when he plunges into yet another self-destructive choice in his erotic and family life.

His personal life proceeded through three disastrous marriages, punctuated by recurrent affairs, before he made an apparently faithful and happy fourth marriage. His public life began with the spectacular success of his first books, lost its way with his later ones, and finally ended in high-spirited political commentary on the hungry left-wing contemporaries of his youth who turned conservative, and hungry for power, in middle age. Kazin knew he could not win his late battles, but died knowing that they were worth fighting. He was both Don Quixote and Sancho Panza, at times tilting against real and imaginary enemies or in ecstatic pursuit of a new Dulcinea, at other times seeing grim political and personal reality when everyone around him was dazzled by self-serving fantasies.

II.

A summary account of Kazin's childhood sounds like the story of any of a dozen Jewish intellectuals of his time. He was born in 1915 to impoverished, mismatched, Orthodox Jewish parents who had emigrated from Poland to the Brownsville section of Brooklyn. His relations with his mother were intense, with his father distant. He lost interest in Judaism, discovered radical politics, attended City College, overcame a stammer, and talked his way into the literary and political world of Manhattan. In his early twenties he was reviewing for the *New York Times,* the *New York Herald Tribune,* and the *New Republic.*

The details of Kazin's life diverge from the stereotype in ways that led to difficult relations with his contemporaries at City College and in intellectual New York. His father had worked in the Chicago stockyards, had roamed the Midwest while working for the Union Pacific Railroad, and would have settled in Colorado had he found a

Jewish girl there to marry. Kazin traced to his father's stories his own love of the American heartland, his identification with every kind of American wanderer. He was more of a literary loner than a political joiner. As Kazin's biographer points out, Norman Podhoretz joined a Brownsville street gang as a teenager; Kazin did not. At City College Kazin thought of himself as a socialist, but avoided the sectarian political fights, fueled by the narcissism of small differences, that notoriously made a battleground of the cafeteria.

On Native Grounds, which made him famous at twenty-seven, was a spacious, enthusiastic history of the previous fifty years of American prose literature in the form of quick biographical vignettes of writers arranged to suggest an extended narrative of social progress. "In a word," he wrote in the preface,

> our modern literature came out of those great critical years of the late nineteenth century which saw the emergence of modern America, and was molded in its struggles.

What was exhilarating about the book was Kazin's ability to use the wisecracking style of an irreverent young rebel as a medium of praise; he aimed his wit at the previous generation of critics who had been too convinced by their own sense of themselves as enlightened rebels to perceive the greatness of those they had rebelled against. The "light-bringers of 1920" had dismissed William Dean Howells as a prude; Kazin saw in his novels the moral and social profundity of an American Tolstoy.

"There is a terrible estrangement in this writing," Kazin wrote. (He meant "the writings I discuss in my book"; Edmund Wilson warned him that his prose lacked precision.) "All modern writers, it may be, have known that alienation equally well." The theme of the book was not literary or cultural exile in a place distant from one's homeland, but "our alienation on native grounds," the condition of being alone in the place where one was born.

A telling moment occurs when Kazin paraphrases Thorstein Veblen on the ability of a Jew to become an intellectual leader by escaping from his native culture and refusing to be assimilated into a gentile one. As an outsider to both cultures, the unassimilated Jew is necessarily a skeptic, Veblen explained, and "the first requisite for constructive work in modern science ... is skepticism." Kazin comments, "It was one of Veblen's rare self-portraits," and Kazin thought it wholly appropriate for a lapsed Norwegian Lutheran to portray himself by describing a Jew.

For Kazin in the early 1940s, Jews were no more alienated than any other recent arrivals in America. For the 1944 survey of young writers' debt to their "Jewish heritage," conducted by the *Contemporary Jewish Record,* Kazin went out of his way to deny that he felt any debt or recognized any heritage:

> I think it is about time we stopped confusing the experience of being an immigrant, or an immigrant's son, with the experience of being Jewish.

This was the same survey to which Lionel Trilling had also given an unassimilated individualist's answer (as did the young Clement Greenberg), but where Trilling tended to orotund vagueness, Kazin was blunt:

> I know how easy it is for the American Jew, at least in my circumstances and of my generation, to confuse his timidity with devotion, his parochialism ... with a conscious faith. ... I learned long ago to accept the fact that I was Jewish without being a part of any meaningful Jewish life or culture.

He also learned, he added, "to follow what I really believed in, not that which would move me through associations or naïve community feelings.... Like many another American, I have had to make my own culture."

When he was writing *On Native Grounds,* Kazin felt (as he remembered it later) a "world-historical sense of purpose," a belief that he was caught up in a great political transformation, a member of "the vanguard on the side of history." He accepted the Marxist assumption that literature was shaped by social forces and class conflict, but beyond a passion for socialism and a hatred for reaction, he endorsed no specific agenda and hated no class enemies. Edith Wharton left him sorrowful, not angry; she was "not a great artist" but at least she was "an unusual American, one who brought the weight of her personal experience to bear upon a modern American literature to which she was spiritually alien."

Kazin was too much of a skeptic to organize the minute particulars of history into a teleological plot, but his sense of historical purpose gave his book its energy and almost gave it a shape. He began to lose his political faith before he finished the book, and by the late 1940s he had lost it altogether. He never found a satisfactory substitute as an organizing principle for his later books. He wrote in his journal in 1947: "What all of us lack more than anything else is a political solvent for our ideas."

By the 1960s Kazin was the most powerful reviewer in America, passing judgment in *The New Yorker,* the Sunday book reviews, and in more than sixty essays in *The New York Review of Books.* He recorded in his journals:

The beggarly Jewish radicals of the 30s are now the ruling cultural pundits of American society—I who stood so long outside the door wondering if I would ever get through it, am now one of the standard bearers of American literary opinion—a *judge* of young men.

Dag Hammarsköld asked him to lunch at the United Nations. John F. Kennedy asked him to lunch at the White House.

His power proved transient. After his death, critics who wrote about him tended to divide into those who called his criticism "indelible" and those who called it "strangely uninfluential" despite its prominence at the time. Both were right. Literary criticism can be influential and memorable when it performs the double function of history and aphorism. As history it tells the unique story of a single book, author, or era; as aphorism it offers a general principle through which to understand any of a multitude of books, authors, and eras. The greatest critics—from Samuel Johnson through Virginia Woolf, William Empson, and beyond—could combine history and aphorism because each had a cohesive ethical vision that made sense of the connections between unique persons and general principles, and between literature and life.

Kazin's criticism was almost all history. In place of aphorism, he offered vague spiritual uplift, as when he wrote of Henry and William James that "they burned with that indestructible zeal we need so badly to recover," or when he underlined his points with incendiary adjectives: "burning," "fiery," "blazing." The experience of reading his criticism is often more "indelible" than anything he actually said.

His memoirs tend to be even more memorable than his criticism, partly because when writing about himself he never felt the same obligation to be factual that he felt toward the writers he revered. He constantly reshapes the facts about his family and his marriages: the same wife gets different names in different books, marriages are conflated, he seems a lonely, only child because his sister Pearl—she married the sociologist Daniel Bell—never gets mentioned. But he does all this in order to portray himself simultaneously as a universal allegorical type and as the boy who grew up in a unique family unhappy in its own way. In his journal he praises himself as a critic in terms that apply more accurately to himself as a memoirist:

> I am…a sentinel of the truly universal experience and far, far closer to the central moral problems in modern literature by reason of my being a Jew, than I can possibly say.

A Walker in the City recalls Kazin's childhood with an evocative precision that both treasures and transforms the tenements of Brooklyn. One typical chapter is a quietly unsettling vignette of a much-traveled Russian woman who discovers the provincialism of the young Kazin with the same wonder with which he discovers her sophistication:

> One day she came into our kitchen, looking for my mother to make a dress for her. I was alone, doing my French lesson at the table. When she spoke to me in her timid, Russian-gruff accent, I felt myself flying back to *Anna Karenina*. There was a grandeur of suffering in her face, in the spindly thinness of her body in the old-fashioned dress, that immediately sent me to that world I had heard of all my life. I was glad my mother was out; I felt I could now enjoy Mrs. Solovey alone.

Only someone who loved Proust as Kazin did could have written this, but the impoverished milieu gives Mrs. Solovey depths entirely unlike those of her more privileged original, Charles Swann.

III.

Kazin's first wife, Natasha Dohn, seems to have been sane, intelligent, and appealing—and resolute enough to refuse to take him back after his first extramarital affair. That affair began after a Greenwich Village party where Kazin met a beautiful young woman with a long history of affairs with writers and artists. She called these lovers her "educators," and imagined she would become more intelligent by going to bed with them, much as young stockbrokers imagine they can become better-looking by going to bed with fashion models. At twenty-eight Kazin was too naïve to know what he was being used for, and too inexperienced to have learned that the all-consuming sexual excitement that he gloated over in his journals can occur only while each lover remains unaware of the other's personality. The affair seems to have ended at the point where such affairs always end: when the lovers finally saw each other as imperfect human beings instead of ideal figures of myth—no longer the Love Goddess and the Great Mind, but Mary Lou and Alfred.

If Kazin's account in *New York Jew* (1978), thirty-five years later, accurately describes his feelings at the time, he never stopped thinking about the affair in the same mythical terms in which it began. She was a "priestess" of love; their affair was a crime he had committed against the whole Jewish people. "I was as bad as any Nazi," he remembers himself thinking. "Breaking up the family—which is what happens with these things—it's breaking up the Tradition." Kazin's breast-beating mythologizing was his favored method of consoling himself: he confessed to a grave fault that he didn't commit so that he could avoid thinking about the lesser one that he did. To betray his people was exciting and daemonic; to betray his wife was merely tawdry.

In Kazin's journals and in all other accounts, his second wife,

Carol Bookman, is visible more as an elegant outline than as a person. Kazin admired her stability and assurance, and never overcame his resentment of her prosperous, assimilated German-Jewish family. The marriage brought into clear focus the invidious hierarchy that divided German Jews from Eastern European ones; the odors of snobbery on one side and resentment on the other are unmistakable in the otherwise apparently motiveless ill-will that divided Kazin from many of his literary and political rivals. Kazin's attempts in later life to find a Jewish identity that could unify him with a coherent group, like other such efforts among other ethnicities, seem to have stumbled repeatedly over the unmentionable hierarchical divisions inside the group itself.

Kazin lived with his third wife, Ann Birstein, for twenty-seven years, most of them miserable. As matters got worse, the two screamed at each other all night over the sound of neighbors banging on walls. Then they settled the argument by enjoying the most intense sex they had ever had since the last time. Much of the misery seems to have been focused on Kazin's indifference to Birstein's novels. In *What I Saw at the Fair* she portrays herself as the passive victim of Kazin's intensifying rage; finally he began knocking her to the floor and once broke her finger when she deflected a blow. Birstein is less passive in Kazin's version, and his journal reports the hair-raising details of their mutual physical and psychological violence, culminating in what Kazin called a "big suicide drama that ended up with the police in our bedroom demanding that I commit her or 'accept the responsibility.'"

Kazin's version agrees with Birstein's in acknowledging that both were unfaithful, that he made neurotic demands for her approval while offering none in return, but he also portrays her as consumed by rage because she blamed him for her failure to become famous as a novelist. She once accused him of "serving on the Pulitzer committee for the sole purpose of denying her the prize." In Birstein's version, Kazin was a monster of egoism, hypocrisy, and greed; but, except for her father and a few walk-ons, her memoir portrays everyone in her life as monstrous in more or less the same way.

Long before the marriage ended, Kazin wrote in his journals about his affairs: "Thank God for Carol and Carla and Rose and Jean, for Celia and Elsie and Sylvia and Rosalind, for Alice and Vivienne—for the other Sylvia, for Lou, Lou, Lou!" Ann Birstein's memoir and Richard M. Cook's biography tell more than I want to know about Kazin's habits in bed, but neither has much to say about the more interesting question of what sex meant to him. His journals—both published and unpublished—make it possible to guess, however, that sex could never relieve his loneliness because he experienced it as an awesome spectacle performed by his body for the solitary audience of his mind.

IV.

In his criticism, Kazin was always alert to a novelist's failure to grant personal reality to any character other than his own stand-in (this was his recurring complaint against Saul Bellow), and in his journals he was often alert to his own failure to grant personal reality to wives, lovers, and friends. Even in his final and happiest marriage he was still surprised to discover that his wife had her own inner life; he records that surprise again and again in his journal, as if he forgot it after each previous occasion. Planning a memoir that he never finished, he imagined himself describing "our transcendentalist so sweetly pious hero, who has not yet sufficiently learned that *there are other people out there.*"

Always sensitive to slights, whenever he met someone warmhearted and intelligent he responded with a gratitude that was near to love. The critic Erich Heller was "a man I like so much and am so attracted to." Heinrich Blücher, Hannah Arendt's husband, was generally condescended to in Arendt's circle (Diana Trilling said Arendt kept him "chained to her bedpost" for use when needed), but Kazin noted his "irrevocable quality" (Kazin often chose a vague word when he was too excited to find a more exact one) after an afternoon of "glorious and strengthening talk."

Kazin's "sickening demand for love and protection" (as he wrote in his journal), his need "for the reassurance of being loved, that is infantile to the point of insanity," was sufficiently sane to make him immune to the counterfeit form of love that is personal charm. In 1961 he began a piece on John F. Kennedy and the intellectuals; Kennedy had invited artists and academics to his inauguration, hired them for his administration, and cited them at every opportunity. Kazin's friend Arthur Schlesinger Jr., hoping he would produce flattering propaganda, arranged for a visit to the White House, where Kennedy applied his charm, which for once failed to work. Kazin's essay portrayed Kennedy as a poseur whose main intellectual talent was his ability to manipulate self-important intellectuals.

Expert as Kazin was at reading character, he seems to have been helplessly naïve at reading social situations. Whenever a college English department failed to invite him back or offer him tenure after a visiting semester, he placed the blame on colleagues' envy of his skill as a teacher and writer. He forgot that he had made a habit of pawing their wives at dinner parties. He loved novels partly because they clarified social relations that he could not otherwise understand, and he wrote in his journal, "The reason I do not write fiction is that I am not yet up to human conflict. I still portray people alone."

His social blindness caused him much anguish when he might have found sardonic amusement. One characteristic episode occurred after the publication of *New York Jew,* when a letter in the *New York*

Times Book Review, signed by nineteen writers, denounced Kazin's portrait of Lionel Trilling (who had died three years earlier) as "a grotesque misrepresentation." Some of Kazin's friends were among the signers, and Kazin assumed he had lost their friendship, and disbelieved those who assured him afterward that they felt just as friendly to him as they ever did. Kazin wrote in his journal:

> I feel humiliated, devastated, etc., by this onslaught against me.... I knew that the Columbia acolytes would organize this demonstration against me, but I did not suspect that so many "old friends" would join in.

Kazin was aggrieved by the letter for the rest of his life, but he got it entirely wrong. Letter-writing campaigns against an author are often about something that doesn't appear in the letter, and tend to be organized by someone who didn't sign it. It should have been easy for Kazin to guess that the letter denouncing him was written by Diana Trilling, and that almost everyone who signed it had no strong views on the matter, but couldn't bring themselves to say no to the offended widow or to whomever she had commissioned to collect signatures. The three signers whom I asked about the incident all confirmed this guess; one doubted he had ever read what Kazin had written about Trilling, and none could remember feeling any animus toward him.

If Kazin had reread his "grotesque misrepresentation" of Trilling, he would have seen that there was nothing objectionable about it. His tone ranged from mildly waspish to gratefully affectionate, and the worst things he said about Trilling were that he was ambitious, that he carefully managed his career, and that he protected himself behind a formal and reserved manner—scarcely shocking things to say about the first Jew promoted to tenure in the dignified Columbia English Department. What provoked the letter to the *Times* was almost certainly Kazin's corrosively accurate portrait of Diana Trilling as a resentful scourge of intellectuals in public and of her husband in private. Had Kazin guessed this, he would have realized that she had confirmed his portrait of her, down to the detail that "her favorite literary genre seemed to be the letter to the editor."

V.

Almost every morning from the age of eighteen until his death, Kazin wrote in his journals his thoughts about literature, history, the social world of publishing, universities, and politics, his marriages and affairs, the "many people I know and admire, or rather love," and what it means to be a Jew. He wrote sometimes as a literary and erotic conqueror, sometimes as a guilty victim of conscience, always with infectious intellectual energy.

He seems to have intended almost from the start to use his journals as a source for his books, a plan he finally put into effect in *A Lifetime Burning in Every Moment*, misleadingly subtitled "From the Journals of Alfred Kazin." (The self-congratulatory main title is a quotation from *Four Quartets*, where it is far less embarrassing.) Much of the book was rewritten or newly written. The journals he originally wrote, excerpted posthumously as *Alfred Kazin's Journals* (2011), reveal the depths of his religious interest, which he had reduced almost to invisibility in his own published extracts.

From adolescence onward, Kazin was engrossed in a spiritual and sometimes mystical inner life. He didn't talk about it, and none of his friends or lovers seems to have been aware of it. His wife Ann Birstein lampooned it in a novel, *The Last of the True Believers* (1988), misunderstanding it as naïve Jewish piety. It was far more hidden than his notoriously florid erotic life. Much of what he had to say in his essays about other people's religion was also about his own, especially when he described an inner faith that rebelled against all churches and doctrines. He wrote in *An American Procession* (1984):

> Emerson was beginning to understand that total "self-reliance" —from his innermost spiritual promptings—would be his career and his fate.

The same thought prompted his journal entry: "*Emerson made me a Jew.*" He was the only reviewer of *The Crying of Lot 49* who correctly recognized it a novel driven by an inward, undoctrinaire religion like his own.

The journals make clear that his long introduction to *The Portable Blake* (1946) was a disguised self-portrait, with Blake's Christianity standing in for Kazin's Judaism:

> [Blake] was a libertarian obsessed with God; a mystic who reversed the mystical pattern, for he sought man as the end of his search. He was a Christian who hated the churches; a revolutionary who abhorred the materialism of the radicals.

Kazin's most energetic essays in his later years were his political jeremiads against neoconservative *arrivistes* who identified their own success with eternal moral truths. As his journals suggest, he was driven to this by a religious sense of what an eternal truth might really be—something demanding, uneasy, uncompromising.

He returns again and again to one central question: how to be a free individual, untempted by convention or ideology yet morally responsible to the unknowable source of all value that it was convenient to call God. "God is only a name for our wonder," he wrote. "We know that supernaturalism is a lie, and therefore miss its truth as myth—as the theory of human correspondences," by which he seems to mean the unseen ways in which individual lives are connected to the larger world. "I am a religious," he writes, using "religious" as a noun like the French *un religieux:*

> I do not believe in the new God of Communism or the old God of the synagogue—I believe in God. I cannot live without the belief that there is a purposeful connection that I may yet understand which I can serve. I cannot be faithless to my own conviction of value.

His pursuit of value and belief takes him to the depths of his private self. "The only meaning of religion is revelation—that is, the meaning and worth of religion come to self-knowledge." His compulsion to keep a journal "is very mysterious," because he writes about himself, but for "someone who is not altogether ME":

> There is a deeper part of myself than the ordinary wide-awake and social one that I strangely satisfy by the freedom I feel in writing this. Some older part of me, anarchistic and spiritually outlaw—that does not have to answer to anyone. Yet demands that I foster it, engage it all the time.

In some of his most moving passages, he remembers walking among the London crowds in 1945, when Labour won the election, and he felt—in what seems to have been an outsider's nostalgic wish for some imaginary lost collective life—a fleeting mystical sense that his individual self-knowledge had hidden roots in unconscious shared experience:

Society, a mass, acting in concert with you, *expressing the deepest part of you,* the unconscious part of you, in fact (just the opposite of being submerged in the crowd). This is the positive sacramental side of society as an institution: working for you, with the energy and unconscious but positive wisdom that you do not immediately find in yourself.

Kazin's journals portray him, unexpectedly, as Emerson's Jewish heir. But he integrated Emersonian self-reliance with socialist sympathies learned from the Labour Party and the London crowds, and from a visionary mysticism inspired by William Blake.

VI.

In 1944 Kazin published an essay in *The New Republic* about the Nazis' murder of millions of Polish Jews—one of only a few wartime essays in mainstream publications in which an American Jew wrote about the destruction of European Jews. After the war, when the full extent of the Nazis' mass murder was apparent, Kazin began to identify himself with Jewishness—not with Judaism as a religion—in a way that he had never done before. He still thought of "the ambiguity and long ache of being a Jew" as central to all aspects of modern culture—Jewish suffering as an embodiment and symbol of everyone's experience, not as a unique religion or history—but he began to experiment with a sense of unity with other Jews, and with a new pride in being one of them.

He exulted at being invited to Israel in 1960, and wrote in his journal soon after he arrived, "Feel very Jewish these days.... I have been seized, I have been pregnant with the Jews." The feeling did not last, and he laughed aloud when his hosts told him that he and every other Jew in the diaspora was obliged to emigrate to Israel. After Israel's rapid victory in the 1967 war, he recorded his "inexpressible pride in our ability to live, to fight it through, to *live*." But when he revisited Israel three years later, he "felt the Jewish obsession...without a lifting of the heart." Part of his discontent was the discrepancy between his longing for transcendence and the coarse, secular, functional society he found in Israel; part, as he wrote in his journal, was that he associated "so much pain, lunacy, and outrage with so many Jews."

Kazin always thought of the Nazis' crime as "the sin of the centuries," but he distrusted any sense of Jewish identity that was built on the fact of the crime—on acts done to Jews by someone else—instead of being based on the actions and beliefs of Jews themselves. He wrote in his journal in 1981:

> Holocaust, Holocaust, Holocaust...The Jews [who] were once held together by God are now held together, or should I say scared together by the Holocaust....And to cap the sin of the centuries, the revived fascists and Nazis doubt that it ever occurred....

Throughout his later work he struggled with his double sense of the enormity of the crime and of the trivializing, self-serving ways in which its memory had been used. Kazin wrote a gratefully praising review of Elie Wiesel's *Night* in 1960. But after getting to know Wiesel in person, he became disillusioned by his "platform" manner, dismissed him in his journal as one of the "actors playing the Holocaust circuit," and finally wrote an essay contrasting Wiesel's testimony with that of Primo Levi, whom he called "a far more trustworthy witness," provoking Wiesel to accuse Kazin of "lending credence to those who deny the Holocaust."

VII.

"Values are our only home in the universe," he wrote in 1962 at the height of his public success, and the more intensely he thought about values, the more intensely he thought about himself as a Jew. "For what is it I draw my basic values from if not from the Jews!" His journals explore a radical, idiosyncratic Judaism informed by the same nonconformist moral passion that drove Blake's radical, idiosyncratic Christianity.

Kazin followed a long tradition in seeing messianic hope as the core of Judaism. "Jews who do not believe in the Messiah . . . are like everyone else and as a tribe not particularly interesting." He had no interest in supernatural beliefs; his messianic faith was his belief in the invisible reality of value and meaning:

> The hidden God. My God is no God shining on an altar in a nimbus of gold-painted spikes, but the hidden God, the God that waits to be disclosed, as we wait—to find him. Between Him and me what silence, what long preparations and rehearsals, what a deep shyness.

All other forms of Judaism are mere vanities. Jews who focus on their collective identity, who ignore "the remote deeps from which their God comes," make Judaism trivial or worse. A Jew must be an outsider, even to Judaism:

> Every original Jew turns against the Jews—they are the earth from which his spirit tries to free itself. . . . The vice of Jewish solidarity—it is an unexpressed* compassion without love. The

---

* "Unexpressed" seems to mean "not expressed in personal feeling."

glory of being in the truth, Jewish or not Jewish, is to find a love higher than solidarity.

Jewish solidarity sustains itself through the conceit that exile and persecution, not faith, define a Jew. The sense that Jews have of themselves

as special cases, as an importunate and eternally aggrieved minority always,...puts them into the position of consciously amending justice and truth in order to get their human rights in....The more the Jews regard themselves as special cases,... the more they keep themselves from achieving this moral centrality, their perspective on the whole human problem, which is their birthright, their privilege, and their real history.

His problem, "as always, is how to be a 'Jew' without 'Judaism'— how to live...without simply becoming a *worshipper*, by which I mean someone bent to *this* cult." What matters about belief is the individual moral commitment that drives it: "not the creed, but the believer." The brief, transforming papacy of John XXIII inspires him to a "sense of moral liberation." John's *personal* faith" gives him a renewed sense that the future is shaped by voluntary moral choices, not by the impersonal force of history:

I am more and more convinced that this dimension of personal freedom...is decisive. Only this individual sense of good and evil can abolish the pathetic sense of being a disappointed spectator and onlooker, a reader of the historical fortunes.

"God is born of loneliness," he writes in a meditation on Melville. The "sense of good and evil" is a universal truth that can arise only from deep private sources—unlike all impersonal generalizations that can be abstracted into a general principle. "The first thing a principle does nowadays, if it is really a principle, is to kill somebody."

In 1962, reading a book of documents of the Nazi destruction of the Warsaw ghetto, Kazin is appalled by a Jewish religiosity that found divine meaning in mass murder:

> Jewish submission, Jewish passivity and quietism. It's as if the phrase used in the ghetto for death at the hands of the Nazis— *Kiddush ha-shem,* sanctification of the [divine] name—expressed the distraction, the God-intoxication, that made everything else unworthy.... Is it really true... that the Jews see themselves (ultimately) as a kind of sacrifice in the divine process of creation?... [What ought to be] the desired condition— pride, resistance, dignity—how is this made impossible by sanctification of the divine name? To believe in the Jews as a necessary sacrifice is to express a nearly Oriental fatalism. In this view the human being is actually held in contempt by God, is nothing to Him, merely exists to demonstrate His greatness.*

What Kazin says about Jewish history is also a response to his family history, to "the anxiety that has been the background of my life, reflected in my parents' insecurity and panic."

The Jews were chosen "to teach all around them the inexpungeable memory of the divine source from which our lives come." That mission, he believed, could be carried out "only in the diaspora, for

---

* Lionel Trilling, writing like Kazin in the privacy of his journals, had recoiled in the much same way from "that vague and masochistic 'testimony'" that, in his view, characterized Jewish culture.

among the nations they served to *remind* the world of the transcendent source and meaning of this experience."

> As a state they can only misuse, exploit, and even kill this mission.... It becomes increasingly clear, as "Israel" ceases to be a faith and becomes an ideology, that Christianity alone does justice to the historic mission of the Jews—that it is only *as* Christians that Jews can remain Jews.

He draws back after writing this, unable to imagine giving up his Jewishness, and adds that a Jew who becomes a Christian "ceases to be a *reminder*" because he has been "swallowed up in the general community of faith. So the Jew must remain in the diaspora...."

To live authentically as a Jew, as Kazin keeps asserting in his journal, is to serve universal justice, to refuse all partisan, tribal, and ideological causes, including those that claim to be Jewish. On Thanksgiving Day, 1988, he writes about "the cry for justice" that rose from the homeless in Depression America and from the Jews in Nazi Germany. But justice is a task for the present, not the past:

> It is plain just now that the cry for justice that comes up very powerfully from Arabs in the occupied territories—and for which over 250 people, many of them young people, have been killed by Israeli army and police—that their cry for justice is certainly louder than that of Defense Minister Rabin talking about the early struggle of Labor Zionists.

The moral individual looks toward the future. "The Christian idea of the future—based on the individual. The Jewish idea: the *past*, the *group*." The Jewish past serves all too easily as a resource to be exploited by the unjust:

A Congressional Gold Medal to Elie [Wiesel]—the whole thing is beginning to stink to high heaven as the most shameless personal aggrandizement in the name of dead Jews.

Meanwhile, he sees "the American Jewish Committee publishing one of the most reactionary magazines in America [*Commentary*], and one which only recently practically justified some of the Nazi murderers among us because of their intense anti-Communism."

In Kazin's journals, an authentic writer and an authentic Jew are much the same. Both are outsiders: not "outsiders and victims merely," but individuals who make judgments based on personal commitment and belief. Both revolt against ideology and convention; both long for absolutes. Kazin loves any writer in whom he sees "the literary radical, the pure Protestant spirit—the individual as consciousness." He is awed by "the terrible and graphic *loneliness* of the great Americans," Emerson, Melville, Whitman, Dickinson, James, Frost, Dreiser, Faulkner, Hemingway:

Thinking about them composes itself, sooner or later, into a gallery of extraordinary individuals; yet at bottom they have nothing in common but the almost shattering unassailability, the life-stricken I, in each. Each fought his way through life—and through his genius—as if no one had ever fought before.

He asks whether his excitement is the effect of his Jewishness: "Is it—most obvious supposition—that I am an outsider; and that only for the first American-born son of so many thousands of mud-flat Jewish-Polish-Russian generations is this need so great, this inquiry so urgent?" Here, and intermittently elsewhere, he writes as if the Jews were the world's only outsiders and that Jewishness has made him one of those "special cases" that, in his more perceptive moments, he reminds himself he is not.

Jewish writers and intellectuals go wrong, in Kazin's eyes, by corrupting the "free powers of the universe" into instruments of their own power. When Norman Mailer wrote about sex, "he betrayed the Jew in him" by transforming a great mystery into a means of "world revolution, ideology, mastership through 'idea.'" The worst betrayers of the Jew inside themselves were the ex-radicals—Norman Podhoretz, Irving Kristol—who now, he writes, proclaim their triumphal servility to right-wing politicians who dislike Jews but are happy to make use of them.

He reveres some, not all, of Saul Bellow's novels. *Henderson the Rain King* "was bad," but *Herzog* "overwhelms me" and *Humboldt's Gift* "amazes me all over again." Like other great Jewish intellectuals, Kazin writes, Bellow sees the world socially from the outside (because Jews are outsiders) and morally from its center (because Jewishness is the epitome of a universal condition):

> This centering in book after book on the individual comes from Saul's sense of himself deriving from the free powers of the universe (the Jewish "God") and from the ability to use the whole social machinery as subject. Emerson spoke of Nature and the me—everything outside me being the Not-Me.... Saul regards the American society as one form that the universe happens to adopt in this hemisphere—and it is the Not-Me.

He is less awed by Bellow the man, "a *kalte mensch,* too full of his being a novelist to be a human being writing," and "congested in his usual cold conceit."

The writer who most inspires him to reverence is Hannah Arendt. In 1963, after reading *Eichmann in Jerusalem*—a book that echoed his dismay over Jewish passivity—he sets her down as "one of the *just.... * She holds out, *alone*, for basic values." Her sense of justice "is the lightning in her to which I always respond." The charged word "gift" recurs in his thoughts about her: "the Jewish intellectual's gift, to see the Christian-liberal-'classical' world from the outside ... Hannah's gift—even when [she] speaks in 'classical' accents." She is a priestess of his radical Judaism:

> When I read her, I remember, for a brief instance, a world, another world, to which we owe all our concepts of human grandeur.... Without God, we do not know who we are. This is what she recalls to me, and for this I am grateful.

Shortly after this, when Arendt's account of the passivity of the Jewish leaders in the wartime ghetto had provoked an angry furor, Irving Howe organized a public meeting about the book which quickly and predictably turned into a hate rally against its author. The event was memorably interrupted when Kazin walked to the podium, said, "That's enough, Irving. This disgraceful piling on has got to stop," and walked out. A recurring note in Kazin's later journals is his irritated sense that those who identify themselves as victims have not had this identity forced on them, but have willfully chosen it because it immunizes them against criticism: any complaint against them can be denounced as a defense of their victimizer.

VIII.

In the early years of his journals, less often in the later ones, Kazin writes in praise of "my honesty and my gift for judgment." Whenever he invokes his own "passion and exactitude and purpose," he sounds like Tennyson's Ulysses, proudly reminding himself that he is

strong in will
To strive, to seek, to find, and not to yield.

Like Ulysses, when Kazin writes in this mood he neglects to ask the crucial question of what he is striving for and hopes to find, a neglect that opens him to intellectual and erotic torments.

"All my life," he writes at forty, "I have been seeking...what may be called the individual strength, the core of maturity, the power to be strong and free inside oneself." He begins to sense why he hasn't found it:

> More and more, it is clear to me that what I suffer from is the lack of a working philosophy, of a strong central belief, of something outside to which my "self" can hold and, for once, forget its "self."...My besetting weakness: an inability to stay with the subject, to devour it through and through.

He never gives up "hope that my inside narrative will yet come to something!!" At seventy-one, he writes: "I work with separate pieces of stone, piece on piece on piece! But I will get the building built."

Kazin gradually became aware that his essays suffered because he was more interested in reporting his excitement than in understanding the book that provoked it. He is nearly fifty before he confronts what he calls

> my tendency as a writer and critic to dwell on the "high-points" of a text, the emotional peaks, the "isolated beauties," instead of the *argument* of a book. My weakness as a literary scholar

and as a writer is to opt for the creative moment rather than for the argument. But only the argument settles anything in a book....

In an earlier entry he had written about "my compulsive need of books, the silent question I ask of myself when I turn to a new one: is it with this that I will be complete at last, lose my long fear of being found out?" This seems to have been the same question he asked himself on meeting a woman, and suggests what he was seeking through his compulsive need for affairs.

When he writes about sex, Kazin forgets everything he knows about individuality. He doesn't want an individual woman. He wants the "secrecy in a woman" that is "the most vexing and yet the most delicious aspect of the feminine principle. It is to this that I make love, and will never be tired of making love." He writes this at thirty-four. He still believes it at fifty-three, when he thinks about a woman's wish to be loved for herself: "How can one explain to her that it is Woman one loves, the feminine principle as the necessity to gratification...." When he recalls his sexual excitement with a wife or lover, he writes as if he had made love not to herself but to her body parts. Finally, at sixty-three, he takes a different line: "The Fool could have learned more from completely loving one woman than he has ever learned skipping from book to book, life to life." He had recently met the woman with whom he made his only successful marriage.

IX.

Kazin's great gifts were those of critical enthusiasm and autobiographical reflection. Both were forms of gratitude. In his middle years, he tended to exchange those gifts for various forms of bitterness. In 1973 he published *Bright Book of Life: American Novelists and Storytellers from Hemingway to Mailer,* an often disgruntled sequel to the often ecstatic *On Native Grounds.* "The novel is the one bright book of life," D. H. Lawrence wrote in "Why the Novel Matters"; Kazin complained that the novel of the past fifty years, "the now chic teachable art object called 'the modern novel,'" through its irony and self-consciousness, had failed to live up to Lawrence's definition. Kazin's second and third books of memoirs, *Starting Out in the Thirties* (1965) and *New York Jew,* substituted thin-lipped resentment for the elegiac depths of *A Walker in the City.* Yet he still believed that autobiography was "directly an effort to find salvation, to make one's own experience come out right."

In the end Kazin found salvation in his fourth marriage and in a new sense of political purpose, accompanied by a new sense of what it meant to be a Jew. The political turning point was an essay he wrote for *The New York Review of Books* in 1983, "Saving My Soul at the Plaza," in which he directed all his exuberant energy against the neoconservatives (many of them his Brownsville and City College contemporaries) who were trying to redefine Jewish group identity as a political movement allied with Ronald Reagan. The title of the piece referred to a phone call from Midge Decter inviting him to a neoconservatives' conference called "Our Country and Our Culture," at the Plaza Hotel. When Kazin said he was surprised to be asked, she replied, "It's not too late to save your soul."

His essay was a joyously devastating portrait of the conferees' infatuation with themselves and their inflated sense of their influence. Kazin understood that the Reagan administration regarded the Jewish neoconservatives as, in a phrase attributed to Lenin, useful idiots. They were invited for dinner at the White House, and, unlike Kazin twenty years earlier, were successfully seduced and manipulated, but for all their preening, they had no power. Kazin, who died in 1998, was spared the less jolly spectacle of the decade after his death, when the useful idiots were invited back to the White House and put in charge of foreign policy.

Kazin's weekend at the Plaza effectively ended his temptation toward a collective Jewish identity. His last book, *God and the American Writer* (1997), was, like his first, a celebratory literary history, based on a renewed commitment to his sense of Jewishness as one of many forms of the lonely search for transcendence that was central to the modern condition and the American experience. "I love being Jewish, but I pursue my own way in these things," he said. "I'm an Emersonian and always have been."

Two months after his essay on the neoconservatives appeared in 1983, Kazin, no longer wishing to dissolve his loneliness in a group, proposed marriage to Judith Dunford. He had made his "own experience come out right," and, though not quite in the way Midge Decter intended, he had saved his soul at the Plaza.

4

MAGUS: WILLIAM MAXWELL

I.

IN THE NINETEEN-FORTIES and fifties a new style of novels and short stories—plotless, undramatic, quietly nuanced, faultlessly phrased—became dominant in American literary fiction. It continues to reign, though less exclusively, in many publishing houses, literary magazines, and creative-writing programs. The "*New Yorker* style" got its name from the stories that appeared there weekly, written by John O'Hara and John Cheever, later by J. D. Salinger, John Updike, and scores of others, some famous, many forgotten. It flourished in American soil because it fed on American myths of detachment as the purest mode of existence and thinking. What distinguished it from the detachment of Huck Finn and Lambert Strether was that it had no moral content, no impulse to escape corrupt entanglements. Its detachment was aesthetic: it treated the world as an interesting place to write about in a tone of calm, cool observation.

This style was largely the work of one man, William Maxwell, fiction editor of *The New Yorker* from the nineteen-thirties to the seventies, and the gatekeeper who opened the pages of the magazine to writers whose style he approved. Maxwell was an almost invisible ruler. He published a few stories in *The New Yorker* and a half-dozen novels, some widely admired, but *The New Yorker* did not publish the names of its editors, and Maxwell's role was known mostly to those writers whose stories he accepted and edited. No other writer in America had ever had anything like this kind of invisible imperial power, and it was made possible only by Maxwell's institutional status. Maxwell never talked about his power—he may not have been fully conscious of it—and the characters in his fiction whom he modeled on himself are notable for their powerlessness. At most, they work in an office somewhere.

Maxwell began his career hoping to become a poet; then he wrote short stories and published one novel before he got his first job at *The New Yorker*. He was a plain-speaking, seemingly realistic writer who wrote autobiographical stories about middle-class life in small towns and urban neighborhoods. At first he tried to imitate Virginia Woolf's lyricism, but he soon cleansed his style of ornament and exaggeration. He wrote in taut, laconic rhythms that evoked the spare speech of his native Midwest, and portrayed his characters' inner and outer lives with economical clarity and nuance. His props and characters were indistinguishable from real settings and persons in Lincoln, Illinois, where he was born in 1908, and Manhattan, where he lived most of his adult life until his death in 2000. Almost every episode in his fiction was reconstructed from events in his life, rearranged for concision and elegance. In a few heightened moments in his novels and stories, he imagined what the furniture and fixtures in a room might say if they could speak among themselves, unheard by human ears, but he presented these moments as metaphors for the sad reality of human moods.

Maxwell had two separate careers as a writer. His first, as a writer of psychologically realistic novels and stories, began when his first novel, *Bright Center of Heaven*, appeared in 1934 and culminated in his last and most admired novel, in 1980, *So Long, See You Tomorrow*. All these books were treasured by a small, sophisticated readership for the quiet perfection of their style and the sad resignation of their content. In the 1940s he began a second career as a writer of magical folktales in the style of Mother Goose and the Brothers Grimm. In these tales the magic hidden beneath the surface of his realistic fiction emerges with explicit and often comic force, and the world of these tales is partly the familiar modern one, partly a timeless fairyland, and wholly his own invention. Readers who admired his realistic work tended to regret the undignified extravagance of his folktales; some wished he had never written them.

Together with his wife, Maxwell became the object of a cult of admirers who thought of themselves as a "magic circle," privileged to have been admitted to an aesthetic élite that gathered in the Maxwells' living room. The Maxwell circle—it was called that from inside and out—was both exclusive and unique. No American writer had ever created anything like it. The closest parallels were the cults that gathered around late-Romantic artist-heroes in Europe: Richard Wagner, Stéphane Mallarmé, D. H. Lawrence. Among his circle Maxwell excited "a kind of astonishment" and "a kind of wonderment"— phrases used by the coeditors of a book of memoirs, *A William Maxwell Portrait* (2004). These editors also write: "There seems to have been almost no one like him in his own time in American letters, perhaps ever." Almost everyone who remembers Maxwell writes about his gentleness and courtesy, and about the extraordinary gifts he made of time, money, and attention. In both art and life, Maxwell was a model of quiet, cultivated discrimination.

Nothing was what it seemed. Maxwell's quiet elegance was the product of a psychological wound suffered in childhood—his mother's early death, his father's quick remarriage—from which he sought relief by practicing the futile magic of art. In both art and life Maxwell's plain style was a mask over a sensibility that had less in common with the chastened realists who wrote the stories he accepted for *The New Yorker* than with would-be magicians such as W. B. Yeats, whose phrases Maxwell threaded into all his work. The world of his serious fiction looks like the real one, but the ways in which things happen there—the invisible connections between events—are exotic and unreal, driven, like childhood fantasies, like folktales and myths, by primitive magic and unseen forces, sometimes generous, usually malevolent. All human acts in Maxwell's fictional world are futile, except the acts of the author himself, the supreme magician—the "Writer as Illusionist" as he called him in an essay—whose memory and imagination can defeat mortality and time.

Maxwell knew how different he was from the saintly image that astonished his friends. He never deluded them into idealizing him— although he never disillusioned them when they did—and he went out of his way to keep no secrets. In the self-portraits he embedded in his serious fiction he is someone who "wants to be liked by everybody," someone who, with deliberate calculation, "lets the other person know, . . . by the sympathetic look in his brown eyes, that he wants to know everything." He gives the forms of friendship, not its substance, because he needs company: "The landscape must have figures in it." In an overtly autobiographical story—about a man who lives, as Maxwell did, with his wife and daughters on the Upper East Side of Manhattan—he wrote:

> There was a fatal flaw in his character: Nobody was ever as real to him as he was to himself. If people knew how little he cared whether they lived or died, they wouldn't want to have anything to do with him.

And in a late story with the pointed title "What He Was Like," a daughter reads her dead father's diaries and tells her husband:

> He wasn't the person I thought he was. He had all sorts of se-
> cret desires. A lot of it is very dirty. And some of it is more un-
> kind than I would have believed possible. And just not like
> him—except that it *was* him.

A wife tells her husband in one of Maxwell's novels, "You have a way of being very kind and gentle sometimes, and of seeming to offer more than you really do." Maxwell's friends, seduced by the flattering sense they got from him and his wife that "you were the most interesting, attractive person they had ever met," overlooked what these fictional self-portraits confessed. Even when a friend writes that Maxwell "could sometimes seduce by idealizing," or when another friend writes that he "had been seduced all over again" by Maxwell's "mystique," they are flattered to have been chosen for seduction, to have warmed themselves from an icicle. Almost every memoir about him includes some variant of the awed and grateful declaration, "I was one of the circle."

"Saintly" is a word that recurs in everything written about Maxwell and his work. But in the same way that his friends ignored the primitive, amoral magic that governs the realistic-looking world of his fiction, they ignored his contempt for any ethical understanding of life—any way of thinking in which actions have consequences, and events are the outcome of human choice, not of arbitrary, impersonal forces.

For those inside his circle, Maxwell's magic brought benediction and comfort, but magic is an instrument of power. John Cheever, a mostly friendly outsider, wrote: "It seemed that he was a man who mistook power for love." A few of his friends were uneasily aware that the magic circle had a guarded perimeter, that its magic was benign only to those allowed inside. One memoir notices Maxwell's occasional "flintiness," but concludes that it was justified: "I never knew him to be unreasonably cold." Among his circle, Maxwell's wound provoked him to sudden acts of cruelty, humiliation, and ostracism, but the effect was to make the remaining members even more grateful to be honored by their inclusion.

Maxwell's realistic fiction comprises six novels and sixty stories. He also wrote forty or more of his folktale "improvisations." His nonfiction includes *Ancestors: A Family History* (1972), about his Presbyterian forebears in Scotland and America, and *The Outermost Dream* (1989), a selection of essays. In the two-volume edition of his work in the Library of America series his career is slightly sanitized by the omission of a few of his stories that the edition does not identify. Most of the omitted pieces can be tracked down by scouring published indexes to *The New Yorker*.* One excluded story, "The News of the Week in Review" (1964), is an acid portrait of a neighbor in Westchester, where Maxwell had a country house. He published the story under the name Gifford Brown, a pseudonym he used when he didn't want neighbors or relatives to notice the unpleasant things he was writing about them. The secular saint revered by Maxwell's friends could never have written it, but the real Maxwell did.

---

* The digital edition of *The New Yorker*, available online and in disk-based formats, contains the full contents of the magazine. The index identifies Maxwell as the author of his pseudonymous stories, but it is oddly incomplete, and fails to list some of his signed pieces. An almost full list may be found in Robert Owen Johnson's *An Index to Literature in the New Yorker* (Scarecrow Press, four volumes, 1969–1976), listed under his own name and three pseudonyms: Jonathan Harrington, W. D. Mitchell, and Gifford Brown.

II.

Maxwell's father, who worked for an insurance company, appears throughout his serious fiction with only slight alterations from Maxwell's memories of him as blunt and remote. Maxwell's older brother lost a leg in a childhood accident but remained athletic and boisterous—one of Maxwell's pseudonymous stories portrays him as a racist boor—while Maxwell himself remained fragile and bookish. When Maxwell was six a young teacher's assistant walked him to and from kindergarten and sang at the family's musical evenings at home, accompanied at the piano by Maxwell's father. Maxwell's mother died in the Spanish Flu epidemic of 1918–19, two days after bearing a third son. He was ten years old. "The worst that could happen had happened," he wrote later, "and the shine went out of everything." All his work is shadowed by her death, which he seems to have experienced less as an event in his personal history than as a condition of the world, like the Fall of Man.

Not quite three years after his mother's death, his father married the teacher's assistant. A year and a half later the family moved from Lincoln to Chicago. "I was removed from Lincoln at the age of fourteen," Maxwell said, "and so my childhood and early youth were encapsulated, so to speak, in a changeless world." He overcame his loss by writing down his memories and preserving them from change:

> I have a melancholy feeling that all human experience goes down the drain, or to put it more politely, ends in oblivion, except when somebody records some part of his own experience.... In a very small way I have fought this, by trying to recreate in a form that I hoped would have some degree of permanence the character and lives of people I have known and loved.

In one of his short stories he wrote of a missing painting: "it is preserved forever, the way all lost things are. It is quite safe from mildew and from the burning pile."

In high school he became passionate about art and literature. One summer, doing chores at an artists' colony in Wisconsin, he was befriended by the playwright and novelist Zona Gale, who gave him maternal literary advice. At the University of Illinois a teacher handed him the newly published *To the Lighthouse*; for the rest of his life he both adulated Virginia Woolf and rebelled against her influence. He planned to get a Ph.D. and become an English professor, but a bad grade in German ended his graduate school fellowship and sent him into freelance work.

He was twenty-five when he wrote his first novel, *Bright Center of Heaven* (1934). It is his only book that remembers childhood happiness as it was before it ended—and as if it had never ended. Years later he refused to reissue it, calling it derivative and, in its mixture of lyricism and cleverness, "stuck fast in its period." These are precisely its charms. He seems to have rejected it because it falsified the past by omitting its overwhelming grief.

The book is an insouciant American fantasia on the first section of *To the Lighthouse*. Mrs. Ramsay presiding over the assorted guests in her summer house in Scotland becomes the motherly Mrs. West at her Wisconsin farm that doubles as an artists' colony. The amateur painter Lily Briscoe is split into an eccentric young artist and a temperamental pianist. In place of the timid couple who get engaged under Mrs. Ramsay's influence, Maxwell's young lovers are an actress and a college teacher who reads Yeats to her and does not yet know she is pregnant. Mrs. Ramsay's triumphant *boeuf en daube* is Americanized into Mrs. West's picnic interrupted by rain.

In *To the Lighthouse* the Ramsays' summer idyll is followed by sudden death and a catastrophic war. In *Bright Center of Heaven* the world of injustice and death arrives in the person of Jefferson Carter, a black lecturer on social themes who is annoyed with himself for accepting Mrs. West's hospitality when he ought to be campaigning against the judicial lynching of the Scottsboro Boys. Before the day is out, he takes offense at a remark that may or may not have been racist, and leaves. Race prejudice is a recurring theme in Maxwell's work, and he later thought he had mishandled it in his melodramatic treatment of Jefferson Carter. But the point of the episode was that a magic circle devoted to art and beauty can preserve its grace and comfort only by closing itself off against harsh realities.

Bright Center of Heaven leaves almost all its story lines unresolved, and the future remains open for all its characters. (After reading the manuscript, Zona Gale wondered whether she had misplaced the final chapter.) The closing paragraphs offer a prospect of freedom and delight: Mrs. West's last thoughts before sleeping are of two birds she released when she found them trapped in her living room: "One of the prisoned thrushes flew into the trees like an arrow. The other cried out for joy." All of Maxwell's later novels, in contrast, end in visions of stasis, futility, and helplessness. His characters, sealed in the amber of their author's sensitivity, have all the attributes of real persons except one: they have no future.

By the time he wrote his second novel, *They Came Like Swallows* (1937), Maxwell had begun working at *The New Yorker,* and had settled permanently into an urban world of hierarchy and power. There was no going back to childhood's maternal comforts, not even in a reverie like *Bright Center of Heaven*, and now he based his second novel on his mother's last weeks at home and her fatal illness in a maternity ward. The title is a fragment from Yeats's "Coole Park, 1929," a poem about an older woman's power to shape and focus everything around her. The story is told from the points of view of Maxwell himself (portrayed as two years younger than he was) and his older brother. The older brother is convinced that their mother died because he forgot to keep her out of the room where the younger brother was in bed with flu. Later someone explains that this could not have caused her death, because she contracted the disease many weeks later. Things happen as they do because life is inherently tragic, not as the effect of human acts. The brother imagines a plot—a connected sequence of events—where there is only a story.

All of Maxwell's novels have a story but no plot. A plot is the means by which fiction portrays the consequences of actions, but it is not like a pool table; one event never mechanically causes another. In a plot each event provokes other events by making it possible for them to happen—possible but not inevitable, because human beings are always free to choose their response to provocation. Maxwell succumbed to an error common among writers who organize their work for the finest possible rhythms and textures: the error of thinking of plot as mechanical and therefore trivial. As he explained to John Updike: "Plot, shmot."

Maxwell continued his life story in *The Folded Leaf* (1945), a novel about adolescence. The sensitive Lymie Peters becomes passionately attached to an athlete in high school. Then, after both go on to the same college, Lymie falls shyly in love with a literary young woman. When she and the athlete fall in love with each other, Lymie tries to kill himself by slashing his throat. The narrator alone knows that Lymie and his friends are doomed to live out patterns unconsciously inherited from a remote past. He describes a fraternity initiation:

> The members of the initiation committee were enjoying themselves thoroughly. They had once undergone this same abuse and so it satisfied their sense of justice. But the real reason for their

pleasure was probably more obscure. They were re-enacting, without knowing it, a play from the most primitive time of man.

His characters experience their emotions as uniquely their own; the narrator dissolves them in vast, tremulous generalizations:

> But to live in the world at all is to be committed to some kind of journey.
>
> If you are ready to go and cannot, either because you are not free or because you have no one to travel with—or if you have arbitrarily set a date for your departure and dare not go until that day arrives, you still have no cause for concern. Without knowing it, you have actually started. On a turning earth, in a mechanically revolving universe, there is no place to stand still.

Maxwell wrote this while he was being psychoanalyzed by Theodor Reik, a disciple of Freud with interests in anthropology and art. Reik believed that a writer's work pointed toward the hidden potentialities of his life. Reading the manuscript of Maxwell's novel, he found a bleak, hopeless final scene in which Lymie's two lost loves visit him in hospital and play childish games with each other's fingers across his blanket.

Reik persuaded Maxwell to add something to the conclusion that would give Lymie a future. When the book appeared in print it had a new final chapter in which Lymie, revived by hope, plants flowers in the forest:

> Although he didn't realize it, he had left his childhood (or if not all, then the greater part of it) behind in the clearing. Watched

over by tree spirits, guarded by Diana the huntress and the King of the Woods, it would be as safe as anything in the world.

It would never rise and defeat him again.

This was false to the rest of the book and to Maxwell's sense of life, but Reik was professionally committed to giving Maxwell a future, not to getting his novels right. For a paperback reprint in 1959 Maxwell restored the bleaker ending.

Shortly after his analysis ended, Maxwell reviewed in *The New Yorker* two of Reik's "courageous and important" books about love, praising him for distinguishing love from sex as other Freudians did not. "Love is an antidote," Maxwell summarized:

> an attempt to reëstablish one's damaged self-esteem by shifting one's ideal from oneself to an imaginary person ... and then to a real person who fulfills the expectations one has had for oneself, and whose identity, after a psychic struggle, becomes fused with one's own.

While he was in analysis, Maxwell met Emily Gilman Noyes, a lively, gracious, Smith-educated young poet and painter from a well-to-do family in Oregon who was teaching in a nursery school in New York and had found her way to his office when she applied for a job at *The New Yorker*. He was thirty-six; she was twenty-three. He had no job to offer her, but he took her to a party and impulsively asked her to marry him. She refused, but, as he told the story later, he kept badgering her until she accepted. What he seems to have brought away from his analysis with Reik was the relieved discovery that he was not doomed by his own hopelessness, that his despair over his mother's death need not prevent him from becoming gregarious, generous, and sympathetic. This discovery about his outer life—with no corresponding change in his inner life—was not what Reik had hoped to give him. A significant few of his later novels and stories portray a man who convinces a woman to marry him and then cannot give her the love she desires. The only life and love that were real to him remained locked in his memory of his first ten years.

III.

Time Will Darken It (1948), Maxwell's fourth novel, is an autobiographical fantasy. Set in 1912, it portrays what should have happened but didn't in 1919 when his mother died. Austin King—Maxwell's father, reimagined as a lawyer like Maxwell's grandfather—has a four-year-old daughter (Maxwell was four in 1912) and his wife is pregnant with their second child. A visiting cousin's daughter stays to found a kindergarten and neurotically throws herself at Austin King. In real life, Maxwell's mother died after giving birth, and his father courted and married the kindergarten teacher's young assistant. Maxwell's own marriage to a young nursery-school teacher in 1945, shortly before he began writing this book, repeated the marriage that dismayed him as a child.

In the novel, the mother survives a difficult childbirth and Austin King is appalled by the young teacher's approaches. In the end the teacher (like one of Maxwell's aunts) stupidly throws kerosene on a smoldering fire, and leaves town scarred and humiliated. The mother is irritated with the father but the family stays intact. Maxwell said he learned from a dream how the novel should end, and its sepia-toned realism masks a child's magical fantasy of vengeance.

Maxwell and his wife made a four-month visit to France in 1948, and he spent the next dozen years trying to write a novel about it. Until shortly before publication, *The Château* (1961) was a leisurely story about an American couple baffled by the character and history of the landlady and guests in the château where they have rented a room. The mostly realistic narrative is interrupted by moments when the style turns magical while the actual events remain plausible. The furniture expresses its feelings:

> *Oh heartbreaking—what happens to children,* said the fruit-wood armoire....The dressing table, modern, with its triple way of viewing things, said: *It is their own doing and redoing and undoing.*

In one harrowing extended episode, the furniture and the characters' reflections in a mirror join in a silent ensemble:

> "My likeness is here among the others," the boy in the photograph said, "but in their minds I am dead. They have let me die."
>
> "The house is cold and damp and depressing," Barbara Rhodes's reflection said to the reflection of M. Carrère....
>
> All the other reflections stopped talking in order to hear what M. Carrère's reflection was about to say.*

Maxwell left unresolved all the mysteries that puzzle the American couple. How, for example, did their aristocratic landlady lose her husband and her money? Maxwell's friend Francis Steegmuller, reading the manuscript to correct Maxwell's French, kept demanding ex-

---

* Silent dialogue was a technique Maxwell learned from Virginia Woolf. This exchange occurs in *Between the Acts* (1940):

> He said (without words) "I'm damnably unhappy."
>   "So am I," Dodge echoed.
>   "And I too," Isa thought.

planations, so Maxwell added an epilogue in the form of a dialogue between the narrator and a reader, in which he waves away the reader's request for the missing links of a coherent plot: "I don't know that any of those things very much matters," the narrator says. "They are details. You don't enjoy drawing your own conclusions about them?" As a sop to the reader, the narrator explains away the landlady's mystery with a melodramatic plot summary that reads like a parody of Balzac. The epilogue answers the reader's questions by insulting him for having asked them. What mattered was the novel's elegance of tone and its pervasive sense that nothing that happens can be comprehended, so nothing can be changed.

As a young man Maxwell had made one deep friendship, with the poet Robert Fitzgerald, a friendship of equals made possible by Fitzgerald's sympathetic understanding of Maxwell's darkest and most vulnerable feelings. In the years when Maxwell was writing *The Château,* as his cultural power increased, he began to attract a different kind of friendship among the happy few whom he and his wife admitted to their circle of admirers. Emily Maxwell now had a career as a painter—one of her portraits won an award from the National Association of Women Artists—and as a reviewer of children's books for *The New Yorker.* Their apartment in New York became a shrine to literature and art, while, for Maxwell, their small circle became an ideal recreation of a small town in the midst of the city.

Maxwell now began to express his faith that writing—the imaginative art of memory—is the highest of all callings. His friends were speaking literally when they recalled that "his religion had been literature" or that, to him, "writing" and "his god...were the same thing." Forgiveness, in his and his wife's circle, was required for aesthetic sins, not moral ones. The tolerant generosity of friendship was less important than the orthodoxy of taste: "Clichés made them wince. But if you were their friend, they would forgive your occasional lapses." Emily Maxwell seems gradually to have adopted her husband's flintiness of judgment, to have become, as Maxwell wrote in his review of Reik, "a real person who fulfills the expectations one has had for oneself." Amidst the circle's elegance and grace, those inside had a quiet, constant sense that they were subject to judgment.

Maxwell had written *Bright Center of Heaven*, with its story of Jefferson Carter's exile from Mrs. West's idyllic circle and its consequent exclusion of mercy and justice. He knew the price that he paid by creating a magic circle of his own, but he was willing to pay it. His friends make vague, veiled allusions to the emotional price his wife and daughters paid for his ascetic devotion to art. "Nevertheless," one friend reports,

> he was unrepentant when he confronted this aspect of his life.... "If I had to do it all over again I don't suppose I would change anything. The writer in me would say, how dare you?"

In the late nineteenth and early twentieth centuries the religion of art was effectively a High Church movement, favoring esoteric doctrines and ornamental, ritualistic styles. By his example, and through his influence at *The New Yorker*, Maxwell founded a Low Church movement with a laconic style and a bleak dogma of hopeless stoicism. Most American priests of the religion of art had exiled themselves to Europe in order to worship in the same High Church with Mallarmé and Rilke. Maxwell's imagination always returned to its first home in Lincoln, Illinois.

Among his circle Maxwell spoke of himself in messianic pronouncements. "I grieve for everybody who was ever born," he wrote to one friend. He said to another: "I saw people all around me, saw what they were like, understood what they were going through, and without waiting for them to love me, loved them." The *New Yorker* writer Alec Wilkinson, in his mostly worshipful memoir, *My Mentor: A Young Man's Friendship with William Maxwell* (2002), was only twice disappointed by him: once over a trivial matter, once because Maxwell had nothing to say when he begged for advice about his failing marriage and his love for another woman. "I knew only that I had asked for help and that he had refused to consider the matter."

But Maxwell had no hidden wisdom that he was holding back. He had nothing to say about erotic and moral choices for the same reason he was contemptuous about plot: he cared about art and the past, not about choices that might shape the future. "The best thing I can do for you is listen," he once told Wilkinson. To his friends, Maxwell was a sympathetic and attentive physician of souls, loved and adored by his patients, to whom he gave opiates because it never occurred to him that they might be cured.

Maxwell took almost twenty years to finish his last and shortest novel, years in which he published two collections of short stories, cultivated his circle, and, in 1975, retired from *The New Yorker*. *So Long, See You Tomorrow* (1980), dedicated to Robert Fitzgerald, is the *summa theologica* of his religion of art. Its story recreates the forgotten events that occurred in Lincoln, Illinois, in 1921, when a husband killed his wife's lover and himself. Before the killings, Maxwell had been casually friendly with the killer's son, whom he calls Cletus Smith. A few years later, in his Chicago high school, Maxwell was surprised to see "Cletus" in a hallway, but passed by silently and never saw him again.

Now, a half-century afterward, he writes a novel about Cletus and the murders as "a roundabout, futile way of making amends" for his silence. He knows his gesture may be futile, but only a priest of the religion of art could imagine making amends to someone by writing a novel about him, in the way that a Mormon priest saves a dead person's soul by baptizing him posthumously into the Mormon

Church. The priest of art summons his congregation to join him in conferring an imagined life on his lost friend:

> The reader will also have to do a certain amount of imagining. He must imagine a deck of cards spread out face down on a table, and then he must turn one over, only it is not the eight of hearts or the jack of diamonds but a perfectly ordinary quarter of an hour out of Cletus's past life.

Maxwell imagines this quarter-hour—and every other episode—with focused inwardness, and renders it in the dignified, conversational style he spent a lifetime perfecting. But his attention never strays from the transforming power of art. In playful moments he imagines what Cletus's dog thinks about the story; in exalted ones he finds solace far from Illinois, in the Museum of Modern Art, where Alberto Giacometti's sculpture *The Palace at 4 a.m.* evokes a vision of imaginative freedom:

> In the Palace at 4 A.M. you walk from one room to the next by going through the walls. You don't need to use the doorways. There is a door, but it is standing open, permanently. If you were to walk through it and didn't like what was on the other side you could turn and come back to the place you started from. What is done can be undone. It is there that I find Cletus Smith.

This was the palace of art that Maxwell had fashioned for himself: princely, ghostly, unchanging, awaiting a dawn that will never arrive.

Reviewers praised Maxwell's fiction for what they called its "wisdom"—which is better understood as a child's desperate hopelessness expressed in the masking dignity of an adult voice. Maxwell had a child's shrewd perception of adult delusions ("People with no children have perfectionism to fall back on," is one of many telling examples), and a child's anxious knowledge of what is lost by growing up. But his novels and short stories suffer from a child's naïve sense that adult life is a series of puzzlingly disconnected episodes, and a child's ignorance of the ways in which an adult's present moment is affected by both choice and circumstance, linked to a remembered past and a hoped-for future.

Yet in private moments, late at night, Maxwell felt safe enough to shed his grown-up dignity and think undisguisedly as a child. He began composing his magical folktales—he called them "improvisations"—a year after he married his wife. Many began as stories he told her in bed; she sometimes had to shake him awake to ask what happened next. At first he thought they were not worth publishing. Then he had some of them printed in limited editions and little magazines, and eventually went public by printing a few of them in the back pages of *The New Yorker*. The one book-length critical study of his work, Barbara Burkhardt's *William Maxwell: A Literary Life* (2005), passes over them in half a paragraph, but they are his most complex and moving works, the ones nearest the heart of his imagination. After his discarded first novel, they are his only works that found their source in childhood itself, not in its destruction.

"Once upon a time," these tales typically begin. Then a talking bird transforms a woman's life; or a family of aristocratic English moles, fleeing modern construction, burrow through the earth to China; or an angry toad curses a child by making her hate her parents; or countries exist where no one grows old, or where all children are born wearing masks that they shed every year. In Maxwell's realistic fiction no one learns and no one changes. In the world of his folktales a queen spends a lifetime learning humility and love, a man who tries to be left alone learns to be treasured by many friends.

Maxwell's imagination in these tales is childlike, not childish, and these quick, deft fantasies shine with a sense of possibility and wonder unlike anything else in American fiction. In his serious writings, as in the aesthetic life of his magic circle, art is the salvation of life, the one certain refuge from loss and change. In his improvisations, art is life's lonely shadow, doomed to timeless desolation, while life, for all its impermanence and loss, can become the realm of love.

One of these tales, "A Fable Begotten of an Echo of a Line of Verse by W. B. Yeats," tells the story of the "monument to Unaging Intellect" in a city marketplace. (In "Sailing to Byzantium" Yeats calls works of art "monuments of unageing intellect"; their proper home is the palace at 4 a.m.) For many years an old storyteller has been telling tales on the monument's steps:

> He had told so many stories with the recognition that the monument was at his back that he had come to have an affection for it. What he had no way of knowing was that the monument had come to have an affection for him.

The storyteller was never a great artist, and now, as he grows older, he tends to lose the thread of his tales. But the monument, doomed to "an eternity of marble monumentality," is grateful even for the storyteller's fragmentary "once-upon-a-times." One day, thinking no one is listening, he tells a tale about the effects of time and change on an old loving couple:

> When the storyteller said, "From living together they had come to look alike," the monument said, "Oh, it's too much!" For there is no loneliness like the loneliness of Unaging Intellect.

The moral and emotional truths that Maxwell's wise-sounding realistic novels studiously deny are the same truths that his wild and naïve-sounding improvisations—freed from his power, released from his circle—triumphantly and movingly affirm.

5

PATRIARCH: SAUL BELLOW

I.

IN ALMOST EVERYTHING he wrote, Saul Bellow asserted his authority as artist, thinker, moralist, and lover. His admirers rejoiced in his authority and celebrated a new kind of dominant voice in American fiction: expansively ambitious, philosophical, and demotic, the voice of a moralizing comic hero unlike anything in the genteel or frontier traditions. "Someone has to stand up for Jews and democrats," he said in a letter, "and when better champions are lacking, squirts must do what they can." His detractors, meanwhile, wrote books denouncing him as a lecherous and corrupt literary tyrant.

Both sides misunderstood him. He asserted his authority half-unwillingly and only as a last resort—because those who ought to be in charge had failed in the job, or had given it up entirely. In *Mr. Sammler's Planet* (1970), he writes:

> Mr. Sammler was testy with White Protestant America for not keeping better order. Cowardly surrender. Not a strong ruling

class. Eager in a secret humiliating way to come down and mingle with all the minority mobs, and scream against themselves. And the clergy? Beating swords into plowshares? No, rather converting dog collars into G strings.

His letters—published a few years ago in a generous selection—make clear what was implicit in his fiction. In one letter, Bellow accepts a friend's judgment that he is an outlaw, but adds: "In outlaw bravado I have no interest. I only meant that I wish to obey better laws." That celebrated rebel Augie March, Bellow explains in another letter, has the same impulse to obey:

> Augie misses the love, harmony and safety that should compensate our obedience.... To me Augie is the embodiment of willingness to serve, who says "For God's sake, make use of me, only do not use me to no purpose. Use me."... Surely the greatest human desire... is to be used.

Bellow was always alert to his position in a chain of command. In letters to a Jewish friend or colleague, he writes from a superior height, either affectionately ("Remember you occupy one of the top compartments in my heart") or contemptuously ("Coventry, pal, is not the place"). To any gentile whom he suspects, usually rightly, of anti-Semitism, he writes in Olympian disdain. But to a Protestant who embodies "love, harmony and safety"—Robert Penn Warren, Ralph Ellison, John Cheever—he writes in courtly gratitude, as he does when he first writes to a future wife, though his tone to his wives changes afterward.

And to Owen Barfield, the English writer of spiritual speculations to whom Bellow offered himself as a disciple, he wrote in forelock-tugging servitude, without noticing that Barfield had no use for it or that he was bewildered both by Bellow's initial self-abasement and by his subsequent revolt against Barfield's authority—which Barfield never guessed he had embodied in Bellow's eyes.

II.

Solomon (later Saul) Bellow was a Canadian, born in a Montreal suburb in 1915 to Orthodox Jewish parents who had fled from Russia two years before, and who slipped illegally into Chicago nine years later. His father had worked in Russia as an importer, in America as a bootlegger and baker. As a child, Bellow spoke Yiddish, English, and French, and memorized biblical passages in Hebrew.

When he was eight years old he came down with pneumonia and peritonitis and began a six-month stay in the hospital. Sixty-eight years later he remembered in a letter:

> Then a lady came from some missionary society and gave me a New Testament to read.
>
> Jesus overwhelmed me. . . . I was moved out of myself by Jesus, by "suffer the little children to come unto me," by the lilies of the field. Jesus moved me beyond all bounds by his deeds and his words.

But he also learned "the charges made in the Gospels against the Jews, my people. . . . In the ward, too, Jews were hated." That hatred was unjust, always to be rebelled against. "My thought was . . . : How could it be my fault? I am in the hospital."* For the rest of his life he was always aware that Christians had betrayed the Christian ideal, and he thought of their hatred of the Jews as the core of their betrayal. They would deserve authority and service had they lived up to that ideal, but, as Mr. Sammler understood, they had failed, and the world was in chaos because no one worthy was in charge.

Most of Bellow's novels contain fictionalized autobiography. Many of his letters include undisguised autobiographical digressions. He was evidently truthful about his interpretations of events, but inevitably unreliable about the events themselves. The shaping power of his imagination kept interpreting the women in his life in a way that led to emotional disaster when they later failed to correspond to his fantasies about them.

His earliest surviving letter is the first of his many anathemas against those who disappoint him. Writing at seventeen to a girlfriend who had found someone else, he tells her, "Yours is a Young Communist League mind." Sixty-six years later, he wrote an ambivalent eulogy for her that made the same complaint in gentler words.

At twenty-two Bellow graduated from Northwestern with a degree in anthropology and sociology. Anthropology excited him. He briefly studied it in graduate school, and dramatized it in *Henderson the Rain King* (1959). Sociology bored him. He listened to sociologists

> with every effort to be fair and understanding but I can't make out their Man. Surely that's not *homo sapiens, mon semblable!* The creature the theologians write about is far closer to me.

---

* In the version of this incident reimagined in *Herzog*, Bellow omits the effect of his reading and remembers instead the "strained and grim" face of the woman who reads the Bible to him; Herzog is five years old, not eight, when it occurs, and can't read for himself. In the version in *Humboldt's Gift*, Charlie Citrine is eight when he goes into the hospital, and "day and night, I read the Bible.... I appear to have become a Hallelujah and Glory type."

By his early twenties he had begun to write letters in the scholar-gangster style that he first deployed in his fiction a dozen years later in *The Adventures of Augie March* (1953). A letter from a friend named Oscar, he writes in 1941, is

> just the sort of letter I have been awaiting from you; one in which you could be a little more recognizable than the Oscar of "cons" and cold-owl trips to see a girl who fucks.

"Cold-owl" alludes to a more poetically erotic trip than Oscar's, Porphyro's journey to Madeline in Keats's "The Eve of St. Agnes," when "the owl, for all his feathers, was a-cold." "Cons" are presumably confidence-tricks.

This style is Bellow's most enduring invention. In all his mature novels, the narrator's voice, rather than the compromising or defeated characters, is the true, indomitable hero. Bellow's vestigial plots exist mostly to give his narrators something more to talk about than cultural complaints and philosophical speculations. His combination of wise-cracking wit and seigneurial authority could not have existed without the precedent set by Damon Runyon's gangsters and molls, whose speech was as artificial as that of the Arcadian shepherds and shepherdesses on whom they were modeled. Bellow transformed Runyon's language into an artificial style suited to an urban-pastoral dystopia, the voice of a Jewish *besserwisser* who could outtalk even the most eloquent gentile. Like T. S. Eliot, Bellow had the characteristically American ambition to master European culture while also seeking beyond culture and beyond ambition for some transcendent spiritual truth.

His pleasure in his own virtuosity is as infectious in his letters as it is in his fiction. Some reviewers of his selected letters complained that all of them were performances. That is precisely what makes them exhilarating. Bellow was most himself when performing, but he never performed merely to display himself. One of the riches of his letters, as of his fiction, is his mastery over an epic range of tone and manner. He calibrates his style to each of his correspondents: to his elders, deferential and ingratiating; to young writers, encouraging and sympathetic; to intimates and friends, either chattily relaxed or volcanically abusive. He writes incidental character sketches as comic and exact as anything in his novels, and when he takes offense at real or imaginary slights, he doubles the force of his contempt by the skill of his rhetorical flourishes.

He tells a friend, "It's harder for me to write the insurance company than to do a story." But his performances left him dissatisfied afterward. He was always troubled by the gap between his peacock's display of words and the self that his words half-concealed, his sense that his bravura was a last resort, a substitute for the security and calm that he despaired of finding. He points in one letter to his "talent for self-candor which so far I have been able to invest only in the language of what I've written"—not in the content. He never stops wishing for a way to speak directly instead of performing. Late in life he describes himself as

> a loner troubled by longings, incapable of finding a suitable language and despairing at the impossibility of composing messages in a playable key.... By now I have only the cranky idiom of my books—the letters-in-general* of an occult personality, a desperately odd somebody who has, as a last resort, invented a technique of self-representation.

---

*An archaic term of etiquette, meaning official or public letters, as opposed to private or personal ones.

Despite these doubts, he represented—more accurately than he understood—his vulnerability, his impulse to trust and revere, his recurring search for what he called strong-minded "Reality-Instructors"—"I bring them out," says the narrator of *Herzog* (1964)—and his defensive fury whenever he feared he had exposed these qualities to others.

III.

Bellow married his first wife, Anita Goshkin, in 1937. The first of his sons (he had one with each of his first three wives), Gregory, was born in 1944. Greg, as he called himself, wrote a memoir, *Saul Bellow's Heart*, contrasting what he calls the "young Saul" of Greg's childhood to the very different "old Saul" whom he became. Young Saul, known only to his family and close friends, was the vulnerable, soft-hearted, independent-minded son of a brutal, observant-Jewish, immigrant father. The memoir begins with Greg at eight, watching young Saul, at thirty-seven, burst into tears after "a terrible argument, in Yiddish, between my father and grandfather." Twenty years later, "old Saul," as his son portrays him, was as rigid a patriarch as his own father had been, humiliating his children and grandchildren in private while denouncing in public the breakdown of traditional hierarchy and obedience.

As a young man, Bellow took sharp pleasure in Jewishness as an intellectual and moral style, a source of irony and independence, but he pulled away from its offer of a collective, ritualized identity. "During those years," Greg reports, Saul "resisted the label of 'Jewish writer,' once pointedly declaring that he liked hockey, but no critic labelled him a Blackhawk fan." Bellow outraged his father by leaving a ham in the icebox and driving on Yom Kippur to visit friends while his family, obedient to Jewish law, walked to synagogue. When his son was twelve, Bellow asked him if he wanted a bar mitzvah, and was content when Greg, whose friends resented being sent to Hebrew lessons to prepare for the ceremony, said no.

Bellow published two novels in a taut, laconic style before he found the courage to go public in his fiction with the style he had perfected in his letters. *Dangling Man* (1944) records five months in the life of a Jewish-American counterpart of Dostoyevsky's underground man, keeping a diary while he waits to be drafted. Like his more garrulous successors in Bellow's fiction, Joseph is alienated from his wife, startled by his own anger, hungry for philosophical answers, and lost in the universe. At the end, he rushes gratefully into the army, writing:

> Hurray for regular hours!
> And for the supervision of the spirit!
> Long live regimentation!

Bellow said at the time, "I was only making an ironic statement," but the irony masks his deeper wish for someone to bring order to his inner chaos.

That wish drives the story of *The Victim* (1947), another Dostoyevskian variation, this one on *The Eternal Husband*. This second novel has none of the expansive self-display of his later ones, but it is far more self-revealing. Asa Leventhal's wife has been away from home tending her mother. In her absence, Asa is psychologically tormented by a down-at-heels New England aristocrat named Kirby Allbee. Allbee has an obscure grievance against him that Leventhal worries may have some half-mad justice. Leventhal is a Jew who nearly convinces himself that a WASP, no matter how repulsive, deserves his service and ought to be in charge. As Bellow did with *Dan-*

gling Man, he spoke of the "ironies" of *The Victim,* and he seems to have been puzzled by what he had revealed about himself:

> I ought to have given Leventhal greater gifts. I'm trying to understand why I showered so many on Allbee instead.

In everything but his gender, Allbee is the first and most fully drawn of the tyrannical, avenging wives or ex-wives who populate Bellow's fiction. Margaret in *Seize the Day* (1956), Madeleine in *Herzog* (1964), Matilda in *More Die of Heartbreak* (1987)—a work of startling misogynistic fury—and Vela in *Ravelstein* (2000) take their distinctive looks, mannerisms, and breasts from one or another real woman whom Bellow married, but Kirby Allbee is the psychological archetype for all of them. The crisis that releases Leventhal at the end of the book occurs when he returns home to find Allbee having sex with a prostitute—a betrayal by a man that serves the same function as a wife's betrayal in novels written two decades later. "You don't care about the woman," Allbee tells Leventhal. "You're just using her to make an issue and break your promise to me."

In 1956 Bellow divorced his first wife after eighteen years of marriage. Four more marriages and three divorces followed. In both his novels and his letters Bellow writes about his marriages—all but the last—as if they were power relations more than erotic ones. Joseph in *Dangling Man* says of his wife Iva: "I had dominated her for years; she was now capable of rebelling." Bellow writes to a friend about his second wife: "When I was weaker there was some satisfaction for her in being the strong one. But when I recovered confidence...she couldn't bear it." (This is fictionalized in *Herzog:* "There was a flavor of subjugation in his love for Madeleine.") Bellow's letters portray a recurring pattern in his marriages. He worships a woman, then marries her; then, a few years later, she reveals herself as the

power-mad fury she had secretly been from the start. It seems unlikely that this should have been inherent in all their personalities;
but in all marriages, each partner's fantasy image of the other has the
Pygmalion-like power to make the image real.

Bellow wrote *The Adventures of Augie March* in "a jail-breaking
spirit" that also motivated *Henderson the Rain King*. But though
both novels are stylistically assertive, their characters yearn to be
obedient and of use. Between these books he wrote *Seize the Day*, his
finest and saddest novel, a brief vision of subjugation and defeat that
renders the bleak world of his early novels in the vigorous style of his
later ones. *Herzog* is a cornucopia of comic protests against the un-
worthy powers, to whom Moses Herzog composes accusing letters in
his head. Those powers rule a society that spends billions on warfare
"but would not pay for order at home." Like Bellow in his letters,
Herzog would prefer spiritual love to carnal love, and wants to write
a book "showing how life could be lived by renewing universal connections; overturning the last of the Romantic errors about the
uniqueness of the Self; revising the old Western, Faustian ideology."

IV.

In outline form, the story of Bellow's inner life is a familiar twentieth-
century story: a young Jewish left-wing idealist becomes an over-
bearing middle-aged reactionary, driven in part by sexual anxieties
obvious to everyone but himself. In its details, the story is far more
nuanced and idiosyncratic, with an unpredictable ending.

The older and harder Bellow who supplanted the vulnerable
younger one was, at least in part, a protective carapace that he built
around himself when he began to feel exposed by fame. He seems to
have regretted revealing himself in the partial self-portraits of his

first two books. The older man concealed his vulnerability and mixed feelings, not only from the public but also, to his cost, from his wives and children. Unlike the ambivalent and self-doubting young father who laughed at his own contradictions, old Saul was abrupt, arbitrary, and uncomplicated. He said what he meant, whether you liked it or not, and became silent when told he was contradicting himself.

Old Saul seems to have taken final form after a crisis in the late 1950s that paralleled the crisis in *The Victim*. Having "kept his head in the sand for an astronomically long time" (as his son reports), Bellow admitted to himself that his second wife, Sondra Tschacbasov, was having an affair with his friend Jack Ludwig. Ludwig had played a fawning flunky to a seigneurial Bellow, and Bellow had taken a teaching job on condition that his vassal Ludwig be hired with him. As in many unequal-seeming relations, the ostensibly dominant figure may not have been the psychologically dominant one. Sondra "maintained that the true passion of the affair was between Saul and Jack."

In Bellow's fantasy in *The Victim*, Leventhal takes revenge against Allbee by pushing him through a door that hits Allbee in the face. Bellow took revenge against Jack Ludwig by writing him into *Herzog* as the domineering hypocrite Valentine Gersbach, "*Saul's* valentine," Sondra said. Gersbach's faults include displays of Jewish solidarity—he lectures to the local Hadassah—of the kind that young Saul despised and old Saul practiced. Bellow defended himself against an oppressor like Gersbach by teaching himself to imitate him.

As a young father, Saul had been, in Greg's eyes, more maternal than Greg's mother. When Saul and the teenage Greg spoke privately, he always asked about the state of what he called Greg's "inner life." Greg once gave him a printed Father's Day card saying, "You've been like a mudder to me, fodder." But the older Bellow swept aside the younger one's respect for his son's feelings, demanding (unsuccessfully) that his grandson Andrew should have a bar mitzvah and learn the religious traditions that he had ignored when raising Greg.

Greg Bellow's memoir recalls incidents when the two Sauls seem to have contended for the right to speak. After Greg reminded his father that he had let him refuse a bar mitzvah, Bellow said nothing more about a bar mitzvah for his grandson, the remembered voice of young Saul having silenced the old one. Soon afterward, however, old Saul, without speaking a word, renewed his demands by sending a messenger, a woman who, on first meeting Greg, "began to badger me about Andrew's bar mitzvah"—one of many occasions when Bellow used messengers and surrogates to impose old Saul's will on friends and family whose memory of his younger self shamed him into silence when face to face.

The old man renounced his youthful internationalism for racial stereotypes and right-wing tub-thumping. The younger Saul, forced underground, remained as rebellious as ever, opposing his own older self as he had once opposed his father. In public, Bellow gave a lecture titled "A Jewish Writer in America"; in private, in a letter a few months earlier, he put the phrase "Jewish Writers in America" between distancing quotation marks and exclaimed, "a repulsive category!"*

In 1967 Bellow got himself commissioned by *Newsday* to report from Israel on the Six-Day War. He seems to have been too busy reporting to write any letters about the war, but he was clearly electri-

---

* The typescript of his lecture includes a rebuke to Hannah Arendt for what he called her "stubborn denial of Jewishness" in her exchange of letters with Gershom Scholem about *Eichmann in Jerusalem*. Bellow misremembered the exchange; she had made no such denial.

fied by its outcome. The Jews in Israel had done what, in his eyes, the WASPs in America had not: they had taken charge; they had put down rebellion, disorder, and chaos. Bellow was not, however, the bloodthirsty hawk he was taken to be after he wrote a book about Israel a few years later, *To Jerusalem and Back* (1976). In *Mr. Sammler's Planet,* no American authority can defeat the black pickpocket who threatens Mr. Sammler by displaying his enormous penis. It takes a half-mad Israeli, Mr. Sammler's son-in-law, to restore order by beating the pickpocket almost to death. But Mr. Sammler, watching in horror, expresses Bellow's own dismay at the needless violence.

Bellow's softer qualities are more or less present in all his books— most vividly in the shorter, less epically ambitious ones like *Seize the Day*—but the old man's genius at self-presentation ensured that the public would imagine him as a colossus like Rodin's Balzac. In his late novella *The Actual* (1997), the narrator seems to share Bellow's private sense of himself: "I myself was both larger and heavier than my parents, though internally more fragile, perhaps."

V.

Bellow was driven throughout his life by his search for some ultimate and invisible spiritual reality. He thought he had begun to find it when, in his late fifties, he encountered Rudolf Steiner's writings about the shaping power of the spirit, and studied him as avidly as Charlie Citrine does in *Humboldt's Gift* (1975). Twenty years later Bellow was still quoting Steiner, whose books, he said, "I've read by the score."

Bellow's most enthusiastic admirers, who celebrate his masculine style or his "Jewish intelligence," are clearly embarrassed by this insistent strand in his writings, and invariably ignore or dismiss it—although his own emphasis on it suggests that their whole perspective on his life and work might need to be adjusted.*

Steiner (1861–1925), inspired by Goethe's anti-Newtonian science, taught that history and nature are shaped by the spirit, that each individual life is part of a single universal process. One needn't believe a word of this to understand why Bellow was transfixed by it. Public and private chaos had erupted because, he thought, no one was guiding the course of history. Marxists in the 1930s had promised that history itself would take charge through the force of violent revolution. Bellow was untempted by that prophecy, but he was grateful when he found in Steiner a peaceful and beneficent alternative, a future in which the spirit would take charge of the world and shape it through inner vision and imagination.

Steiner's greatest English disciple was Owen Barfield (1898–1997), a lawyer and critic who was a close friend of C. S. Lewis and J. R. R. Tolkien. In 1975, shortly before he turned sixty, Bellow read Barfield's *Unancestral Voice* (1965), in which an English lawyer named Burgeon comes across a book about a sixteenth-century Jewish mystic through whom an inner voice, the Maggid, spoke in Hebrew about ultimate realities. Burgeon soon begins to hear an inner voice speaking to him in English about ultimate realities. He names it the Meggid because it is both like and unlike the one that spoke four centuries earlier. The Meggid is the servant of great spiritual forces whom it names Gabriel and Michael. On their behalf it explains how the

---

* Frank Kermode's comment on an apparently irrelevant passage in *The Tempest* provides a model for any reader embarrassed at some aspect of a great writer's work: "It is a possible inference that our frame of reference is badly adjusted, or incomplete, and that an understanding of this passage will modify our image of the whole play."

spirit has created and shaped the material world, how it transforms everything from quantum physics to human sexuality, and how its greatest transforming act was the incarnation of Christ.

Bellow found in Barfield's book what he had found in himself: a Jewish inner voice proclaiming a Christian mystery. He wrote to Barfield to ask for a meeting: "I'd be very grateful for the opportunity to talk to you about the Meggid and about Gabriel and Michael and their antagonists.... I am, I assure you, very much in earnest." A few days later he flew to London. Barfield came down from Kent to meet him.

Barfield (whom I happened to meet soon after these events) embodied, in a quietly memorable way, serenity and invulnerability. These were the same qualities that provoked Bellow to erotic worship when he found them in a young woman. His letters to Barfield display an almost stammering discipleship unlike anything else in his life. "This makes little sense to you perhaps." "I'm a bit ashamed to present such a picture of confusion." "It is all too bewildering."

Bellow's relations with Barfield over the next few years, as recorded in his letters, read like a muted version of his first four marriages. After a period of deference, he protests against Barfield's slights, criticizes Barfield's deficiencies as a master, and declares his independence—although he never explicitly breaks off relations and remains courteous even in rebellion. The one reviewer of Bellow's *Letters* who noticed this incident called Bellow's revolt "a stirring moment.... He will have no more of the other side's condescension to this side."

This episode, like Bellow's marriages, appears in the edition of Bellow's letters only in the form of Bellow's side of the story. But Bellow's relations with Barfield, unlike his marriages, are documented elsewhere from both sides. The entire interchange was published in a biography of Barfield by Simon Blaxland-de Lange,* and it tells a very different story from the one suggested by Bellow's letters alone.

After their first meeting, Bellow writes deferentially, accepting what he took to be a rebuke:

> It must have struck you as very adolescent. You asked me how old I was. "Sixty," I said. Then you smiled and said, "Sixteen?" It was the one joke you allowed yourself at my expense, and it was entirely justified.

Barfield answers:

> You evidently read into that "sixty" and "sixteen" exchange a whole lot of meaning that simply wasn't there. All that actually happened was that I did for an instant actually hear "sixteen" and thought the error ludicrous enough to be worth sharing.

Barfield admits he wasn't "held by" *Humboldt's Gift,* but he blames himself: a child of the Victorian era, he has limited tastes and can't see what everyone else sees. He had the same difficulty with a book by another friend, *The Lord of the Rings*. He knows he may be more jealous of Bellow's success than he consciously perceives, but he is baffled by the intensity of Bellow's reaction:

> I doubt if you have been much more troubled by anything I have said about your novels than I was by what you say about its effect on you. You speak of my judging them. I thought I had made it clear that I did not feel confident enough to do anything

---

* *Owen Barfield: Romanticism Come of Age: A Biography* (Forest Row: Temple Lodge, 2006).

of the sort. . . . I still do not understand how you can have got the impression that I found anything "false" either in *H. G.* or anything else I read. Not the shadow of a dream of anything of the sort.

Maybe you have not fully realized what a Nobel prizewinner feels like from outside. I wrote as breezily as I did because I supposed that any lack of appreciation from this quarter could do about as much damage as a peashooter will do to an armoured car.

A few years later, Barfield reviewed *The Dean's December* (1982) in an obscure magazine. He quoted the autobiographical hero's report of his Steinerian interests: Corde, the dean, Bellow wrote, "was, more or less in secret, serious about matters he couldn't even begin to discuss . . . for instance, the reunion of spirit and nature (divided by science)." But Barfield wondered whether Corde's "extreme interior self-awareness" and "abnormally vivid external" awareness held him back from a "leap beyond" them to the reunion that he sought.

These were also Bellow's questions, but he wrote a courteously defensive response, telling Barfield he was perhaps too English to understand that Corde's self-consciousness was a form of passion. Corde is militantly angry at American society, "but he is far more concerned to purge his understanding of false thought than to protect himself." One could only take the "leap beyond," Bellow continued, if one had "dependable and certain knowledge of what the leap will carry you into"—and then, realizing that "certain knowledge" about the spirit was impossible, he added:

"Certain knowledge" isn't it either, but it would have to be a leap into a world of which one has had some experience. I have had foreshadowings, very moving adumbrations, but the whole vision of reality must change in every particular and the idols dismissed. Then one can take flight.

Corde's passionate anger is his last-resort substitute for the mystical flight he is too earthbound to attempt.

VI.

Greg Bellow felt as if he lost his father twice while he was still alive. The first loss occurred when he left Anita, Greg's mother, in 1952. The second occurred in the 1960s when the newly conservative Bellow repudiated the freethinking ideals that he had taught Greg in childhood. Greg became a psychotherapist specializing in unhappy children. "Saul commented that I had turned the misery of my childhood into a career."

After the first loss, Greg still found comfort in his father's visits and care, and when Anita, having remarried, spent Greg's college fund furnishing a new house, Saul took over her share of the expenses. After the second loss, the relations of father and son took two conflicting forms. At times they shared intense emotional intimacy and wept together at deaths among family and friends. At other times, they withdrew into tense silences. One lasted eighteen months, after Saul, having said he was "moving heaven and earth" to attend Greg's daughter's wedding, curtly announced that he would not be there. Greg and his daughter "had a heart-wrenching conversation about how Saul could inflict so much pain by making commitments and failing to fulfill them."

What prompted Greg to write his memoir was his discovery, after his father's death, that Saul had accumulated a vast family of literary heirs in addition to his biological ones. These literary heirs remembered an ideal father entirely unlike Greg's real one. This discovery felt like yet another loss of his father.

In death, Saul had been taken over, it seemed, by an efficient and impersonal public relations machine. Bellow's lawyer reported his death to the news media, not to his children. Greg first heard of it from his car radio. No one from Bellow's real families was asked to speak at his funeral. He was memorialized instead by a writer, "the literary 'son,'" and an academic, "the dutiful Jewish 'daughter.'" Afterward, Greg read published tributes—in which "I could barely recognize Saul"—by younger writers declaring their spiritual intimacy with his father:

> In the following weeks I heard and read many anecdotes and accounts that claimed a similar special closeness with Saul Bellow the literary patriarch. I took them to be distinctly filial and soon came to feel that dozens of self-appointed sons and daughters were jostling in public for a position at the head of a parade that celebrated my father's life. By now irked by the shoving match at the front of the line, I asked myself, "What is it with all these filial narratives? After all, he was *my* father! Did they all have such lousy fathers that they needed to co-opt mine?"

Greg names three writers for whom Bellow was a literary father, all of whom wrote books prompted by their vexed relations with their real fathers.

The relation between a literary father and a literary heir is always one of mutual idealization. Similar cross-idealizations of *éminence terrible* and *enfant gris* occur in other fields and in both sexes. The most common variety seems to be prompted by a young person's wish to find a mentor, a word that points directly to the fantasy behind the wish. In the *Odyssey*, the Ithacan elder Mentor is not a mentor at all; the protective guide who takes Telemakhos in hand is Athena disguised as Mentor, a divinity filling a role that no ordinary mortal could manage.

Not all celebrated writers attract idealizing literary children. Those who do seem to have an unusually sharp divide between their public image and their private self, between their versions of old Saul and young Saul. Another writer who attracted many ideal sons (one was also an ideal son to Saul Bellow) was Lionel Trilling, whose amoral, nihilistic inner self kept resolving to repudiate his outer self's "character of public virtue." Instead, he repudiated, one after another, the ideal sons who were mirror images of it.

What the literary father seems to find in an ideal son is an image of his younger self as it might have been without its weakness and doubt, the younger self whom Saul Bellow unhappily remembered whenever Greg came to visit. What the literary son finds in an ideal father is an image of what he might become if he could overturn the barriers left inside him by his real father. Each wants the other to provide a relief from anxiety that no idealizing fantasy can give; so the claims of sonship that so annoyed Greg Bellow remain frequent and insistent.

Greg Bellow's often angry relation with his father was evidently one of mutual love, while the seemingly harmonious relations between literary fathers and their ideal sons are always ones of mutual use. Christopher Isherwood, another hero for younger writers, noted in his diary that one's "warmest supporters are the ones who do the most...to make you look ridiculous." Bellow's literary heirs tend to celebrate him in absurdly heroicizing ways, and they invariably quote the verbal fireworks that make him dazzling—the long propulsive sentences, accumulating phrase upon gorgeous phrase like a street-wise Walter Pater—not the laconic evocations of loss, especially in shorter books like *Seize the Day*, that make him moving.

Bellow's heirs like to imagine him as a nineteenth-century artist-hero, beyond good and evil, exempted from all other obligations through the service demanded by his art. One reviewer who savaged Greg Bellow's book argued that Saul had

> struggled to create something out of nothing, and had to justify that scandalous magic in conventional, unmagical, mid-century America. This justification expressed itself all too often as self-justification, and the storm of assertion cleared a brutal path.... In two or three generations, that story will have faded from memory, outlived by what it enabled.

It was of course Bellow's brutal actions that "cleared a brutal path," not his self-justifying "storm of assertion" about them, and these sentences argue for a fantasy of writing as a "scandalous magic," a godlike creation ex nihilo (a "nothing" that was in fact crowded with living wives and friends), and a fantasy of brutality as something that only the boring and bourgeois recoil from. Like all immoral arguments, it is also illogical, relying as it does on the *post hoc ergo propter hoc* fallacy that Bellow's brutality "enabled" his writing rather than coexisting with it or diminishing it. Had Bellow done less damage in life he might have written even better novels, without the preening and point-scoring that disfigure most of his later books.

In his last years, Bellow became increasingly aware of what he had lost through his fantasy of patriarchal strength, and increasingly convinced that young Saul had been right all along. In his mid-eighties he astonished Greg by announcing, "I should never have divorced your mother." Greg responded with the same *l'art pour l'art* defence later adopted by Bellow's literary heirs:

Flabbergasted, I expressed my doubt that he could have written his novels without divorcing Anita and pursuing the more independent life of a writer. He brushed my objections off....

Bellow was not speaking merely for Greg's benefit. He seems to have been in the same frame of mind a few years earlier when he wrote *The Actual*, the brief, austere masterwork of his old age, published when he was eighty-two. The narrator, Harry Trellman, understands at last that the only woman who is real to him is Amy Wustrin (Bellow scarcely bothers to disguise her origins in Anita Goshkin), whom he had dated briefly in high school but never pursued further because, as she now reminds him, fifty years later, "your classification for me was 'a petty-bourgeois broad.'" Each married someone else; years passed without them seeing each other; Harry failed to recognize her once in the street. Now he writes, in the voice of young Saul undoing old Saul's errors:

We had gotten along for decades without each other. Separate arrangements were made. All the while, I had concluded that I was too odd for her. Or that for various other reasons she assumed I could never be domesticated. So my emotions went into storage, more or less permanently. But by and by I began to see what sort of hold she had on me. Other women were apparitions. She, and only she, was no apparition.

Amy is "the actual": "Other women might remind me of you, but there was only one actual Amy." The best way he can think of to describe his love, he says, is to call it "'an actual affinity.'" Trellman is well-read—he mentions Jowett's Plato, Gibbon, Freud, Stanislavsky—and doesn't need to explain that he is adapting an old scientific vocabulary to describe a love that connects one specific individual to another, as opposed to "elective affinities"—the title of Goethe's bleakly deterministic novel about the erotic relations that one generic type of person tends to fall into when placed in proximity with another generic type.

The Actual returns after forty years to the emotional landscape of *Seize the Day*—a younger man letting himself be guided by an unseeing and unreliable older one—and changes it. Tommy Wilhelm, in *Seize the Day,* ended the day weeping over a stranger's coffin. Harry Trellman, in the last sentence of *The Actual,* proposes marriage to Amy Wustrin. "This is the time to do what I'm now doing, and I hope you'll have me." The book ends before she answers.

In Bellow's earlier novels, as in his final one, *Ravelstein,* his fictional self wanted a woman's uncritical, approving love, and knew for certain whether or not she had given it. He wanted the same thing in his marriages. What he hopes for in the last words of *The Actual* is a very different kind of love—neither uncritical nor approving, but forgiving, and he does not pretend to know whether it will be given to him. But it may be relevant to his hope of reversing the past that Harry, a few moments earlier, watched gravediggers raising the coffin of someone whose "theatrical will" had been "to come back from the grave." The young Saul, part of him still the eight-year-old boy in the Montreal hospital who had absorbed many words about forgiveness and hope, survived in the patriarch. "A well-worn copy of the New Testament," Greg writes, "was on Saul's bedside table during his final illness."

VII.

In his last years, Bellow found at least some of the serenity he had been searching for. He seems to have experienced his fifth marriage, to Janis Freedman in 1989, as, in some paradoxical way, a marriage of equals. She was forty-four years younger and had worked as his secretary, but Bellow's sense of age and weakness seems to have balanced his status and authority. Two months after they married he wrote to a friend:

> I am not one of Janis' problems, nor is she one of mine. Perhaps this shows that only an odd marriage can be a happy one. Janis speaks of us as an old married couple. I suppose this breaks down as: I am old, we are married.

His last novel, *Ravelstein*, was his slightest—serenity came at a literary price—but it unexpectedly revived his old comic energy. It has a tone of uncompetitive sweetness unlike anything in his earlier books, and he no longer felt the old expansive impulses that had driven them:

> It's difficult for me now to read those early novels, not because they lack interest but because I find myself editing them, slimming down my sentences and cutting whole paragraphs.

The last thing Bellow wrote seems to have been a letter he sent to a friend a year before his death in 2005, at eighty-nine. It ends in a Proustian reverie about his childhood, prompted by his "pleasantest diversion," playing with the four-year-old daughter born to his fourth wife:

> My mother coveted for me a pair of patent-leather sandals with an *elegantissimo* strap. I finally got them—I rubbed them with butter to preserve the leather. This is when I was six or seven

years old, a little older than Rosie is now. Amazing how it all boils down to a pair of patent-leather sandals.

I send an all-purpose blessing...

Serenity, like love and sleep, evades its pursuers. But it lets itself be found in a congenial marriage and a memory of childhood.

6

MYTHMAKER: NORMAN MAILER

I.

NORMAN MAILER WAS sixteen when he discovered John Steinbeck, John Dos Passos, and James T. Farrell and, he said later, "formed the desire to be a major writer." He was twenty-five when his first novel, *The Naked and the Dead* (1948), made him famous for its narrative force and notorious for its army barracks vocabulary. He became the most celebrated and most reviled American writer of his time, a one-man industry producing stories, novels, poems, sportswriting, essays, histories, and biographies in expansive and exhilarated prose; directing films and plays; making headlines with his eloquent protests against the Vietnam War, his quixotic campaign to be mayor of New York, his outrageous theories of race and sex, his skill as an amateur boxer, his six marriages and uncountable affairs, and the drunken fights, in one of which, on a bourbon-and-pot-addled night, he stabbed his second wife almost to death.

He hoped to write a novel great enough to cause "a revolution in the consciousness of our time." But his best work was his political and cultural reportage: *The Armies of the Night* (1968), *Miami and the Siege of Chicago* (1968), *Of a Fire on the Moon* (1971), and *The*

Executioner's Song (1979). He insisted on marketing the last of these as fiction, although he said it was "a factual account...as accurate as one can make it." He spent much of his life reporting facts as if he were writing fiction, and performing—for an audience of gossip columnists and shockable reviewers—a fictional version of his life as though it were fact.

Mailer wrote prolifically about gods, devils, and divine forces, and his homegrown varieties of gnosticism and kabala were at the heart of his work—from the intimations of obscure powers in *The Naked and the Dead* to the devil who narrates *The Castle in the Forest* (2007). He had, he said, the "mind of an outlaw," but an outlaw whose whole career was a quest for transcendence. The sixteen-year-old Harvard freshman who hoped to be an aeronautical engineer became the mystical prophet thundering against technology—plastics, synthetics, birth control, computers—as a form and cause of cancer in individuals and nations. His last book was *On God: An Uncommon Conversation* (2007), a transcript of talks with his literary executor Michael Lennon.

The same habits of mind that kept Mailer from writing a great novel made him a great journalist. He was less interested in human beings—their personal qualities, their social relations—than in the quasi-divine forces they embodied, and in the vast unconscious currents that shaped political and cultural history. Even in his most florid writing about sex he was excited above all by the mystical powers incarnated in the hydraulic body parts he portrayed. When he talked about religion he sounded like the village gnostic, but he meant what he said. "God was...at war with the Devil," he wrote in *Of a Fire on the Moon* and elsewhere. He told Lennon: "It makes sense to me that this strife between God and the Devil has been a factor in evolution." "When we act with great energy," he said, "it is because God and the Devil have the same interest in the outcome."

He was not being metaphorical. He imagined the devils in *The Castle in the Forest* as fictional characters like Anna Karenina, semidivine persons who don't exist but resemble those who do.

The best of Mailer's novels after his first—*The Deer Park* (1955), *Why Are We in Vietnam?* (1967), *Harlot's Ghost* (1991)—display more variety of style and incident than whole generations of novelists normally achieve. But even these novels go more or less wrong because he imagined his characters more as embodiments of impersonal forces than as persons. He planned a series of novels in which characters from *The Deer Park* would reappear in each book transformed into different persons, sometimes as a reincarnation of an earlier self, sometimes taking their form from powers they encounter on their mystical journey at "some lost way-station of the divine."

Mailer said that his novel about reincarnating pharaohs, *Ancient Evenings* (1983), was set in a world "before anything we know," "without Moses or Jesus," though not, apparently, without C. G. Jung or Joseph Campbell. All the major characters are mythical archetypes—or twentieth-century notions of archetypes—temporarily occupying one or another human body, reincarnating themselves through vaginal sex, probing mystic depths through anal sex with women and men. A narrator-prince, waking into death, opens the book by saying, "Crude thoughts and fierce forces are my state," summarizing Mailer's idea of ultimate human reality. Mailer's own state tended to be the theoretical speculation and bourgeois work habits that generated his enormous output.*

He wanted to be the kind of writer who could "seize the temper of our time and turn it"—the phrase he used to describe the kind of

---

* Mailer appended scholarly bibliographies to some of his later novels, typically listing a hundred or more books, with the most useful ones starred. The bibliography for *The Castle in the Forest* includes (for example) the *Niebelungenlied* and books by Mann and Heidegger.

writer that Saul Bellow, he predicted, was unlikely to become. He seems never to have said he planned to write the Great American Novel—Dos Passos, he said, had come closest to that goal with the three volumes of *U.S.A.*—but he shared that peculiarly American fantasy with many of his contemporaries. The American idea of a novel that transforms its era depends on a corollary fantasy about the writer-hero, the solitary genius who gathers in himself the wishes of a vast undifferentiated multitude, a figure whom Mailer kept dreaming about but only found among politicians and champion athletes. No European writer imagines writing the Great English or French or German Novel because the great theme of European literature is the mutual relation of individual persons with each other and with the differentiated hierarchy of the social world—a set of relations that never dissolve into a great mass that one hero can embody. The European novel always exists in dialogue with other novels. The Great American Novel—if it could ever actually exist—would stand alone in its capacious greatness.

Mailer made a deliberate choice, he said, never to write about his childhood. As a result, he wrote only about experiences that had been mediated through adolescent theorizing or adult intelligence, never the unfiltered feelings of a child. The narrator of his second novel, *Barbary Shore* (1951), is an amnesiac who seems to have been a college student and soldier but otherwise suffers what Mailer described in his own life as a "lobotomy to my past." Mailer's hero D. H. Lawrence wrote of James Joyce's later work that it was "too terribly would-be and done-on-purpose, utterly without spontaneity or real life." Mailer's later novels tend to be done-on-purpose products of will, unsoftened by the gifts of memory and written in defiance of his deepest sense of himself: "I, who am timid, cowardly, and wish only friendship and security," he wrote in a journal, "am the one who must take on the whole world."

The archetypal impulse that blurred and abstracted his fictional characters made his political reportage vivid, focused, and convincing. Unlike every other political writer of his time, Mailer understood instinctively and sympathetically—not through sober analysis —that political trends were driven by irrational collective myths, that the public saw political leaders as embodiments of mythical heroes. In his essay on John Kennedy's presidential campaign, "Superman Comes to the Supermarket,"* he wrote: "There is a subterranean river of untapped, ferocious, lonely and romantic desires, that concentration of ecstasy and violence which is the dream life of the nation."

Everyone read this as a vivid metaphor. Mailer, like a nineteenth-century romantic nationalist, meant it literally. He always believed that a nation such as the United States or a people such as "the Negro" had a psyche of its own, with "unconscious undercurrents" that shaped its destiny. "Minority groups," he wrote, again literally, "are the artistic nerves of a republic." He believed in myths that, like all great myths from Zeus to the modern myth of an impersonal "society" that wields Zeus's omnipotence, seemed to make literal sense of reality. A myth, for someone who believes in it, is not myth but truth.

Mailer's accounts of political conventions, campaign tours, boxing matches, protest marches, and swarming journalists are his most memorable essays and books. He typically presents himself as an archetypal figure, "the reporter," "the novelist," "the observer," "Aquarius," or some other avatar of the writer-hero with a thousand faces. The boxers, politicians, and tycoons whom he reported on were equally archetypal, but he also perceived, sometimes belatedly, that a mythical hero could be the mask of a calculating operator. Marilyn Monroe said of his Hollywood novel *The Deer Park* that he

---

* With his craftsman's sense of euphony, Mailer preferred his original title, "Superman Comes to the Supermart," to the title imposed on him by an editor at *Esquire*.

was "too impressed by power," and he portrayed Kennedy the candidate as the World Spirit in an open-backed convertible. But when Kennedy was elected a few weeks later, Mailer, fearing he had apotheosized an opportunist, "felt a sense of woe."

Mailer wrote relatively little criticism, but his reviews of books and films have an unforced enthusiasm unlike anything else in his work. His love for his craft was his fiercest erotic passion. His critical essays celebrate or excoriate his fellow craftsmen, and he enjoyed gathering a crowd of them in a single essay for mass distribution of praise and blame. (Craftsmen only: "I have nothing to say about any of the talented women who write today," he wrote, to avoid saying they bored him.) Two essays, "Quick Evaluations on the Talent in the Room" and "Some Children of the Goddess," are cheerful bumper-car mêlées, including some assaults on books he admits he hasn't read but is certain will be bad. He wrote a scene-by-scene dissection of *Last Tango in Paris* somewhat in the mood of Shakespeare's Theseus delighting in the earnest awfulness of *Pyramus and Thisby*. He had a habit of slipping literary-critical judgments into his essays on other subjects entirely. In one of his long denunciations of modern synthetics, written in his best prophetic style, he listed "fiberglas, polyethylene, bakelite, styrene, styronware." The last of these was the trade name he invented on the spot for William Styron's novels.

Mailer was unique in combining mythological imaginings with left-wing politics. Writers like W. B. Yeats and Ezra Pound who saw the world through archetypal myths tended to favor reactionary fantasies about natural hierarchies and golden-souled leaders. Writers tempted by archetypes but who refused the temptation, like Virginia Woolf and W. H. Auden, aligned themselves with the rational, egalitarian left. Mailer was a mythologizer who was passionate against injustice, and his double perspective opened his way to become the first American who was able, on occasion, to write about his country with the prophetic depth and precise observation of a Tocqueville.

Mailer did his best reporting in the 1960s, when American politics resembled a Wagnerian apocalypse. He had less to say, and felt "much out of step," from the 1970s to the 1990s, when cynical technocrats took charge and politics seemed opaque to the mythical imagination. Then, on September 11, 2001, he wrote soon afterward, "gods and demons were invading the US, coming right in off the TV screen. . . . It was as if untold divine forces were erupting in fury." As the Bush administration began shining its costume armor for a new crusade, Mailer, now in his seventies, wrote again with all his old energy and insight.

Much of the political left explained the Iraq war as Kissingeresque realpolitik; Mailer, while acknowledging that a thirst for oil was part of the story, recognized the theological impulses that drove Bush, Rumsfeld, and Wolfowitz because those impulses were distorted versions of his own. The "undisclosed logic" at "the root of flag conservatism" was theological: the "militant Christian" belief that America is "the only force for good that can rectify the bad," the "unspoken desire to go to war" felt by half of America because "it satisfies our mythology. "

"Myths are tonic to a nation's heart," Mailer wrote, but "once abused . . . they are poisonous." Sometimes he was the abuser. He wrote an essay that made all the rational and moral arguments against capital punishment with force and clarity, but concluded that state-sponsored killing "may be one of our last defenses against the oncoming wave of the computer universe."

The Executioner's Song is the best of his books partly because he forced himself to hold back from mythologizing and write about murder and misery in a stark, almost unornamented style. Joan Didion observed that the first half of the book was spoken mostly by women constrained to a local domestic world, the second half by men "who move in the larger world and believe that they can influence events."

Mailer acknowledged that she was right, although he had mistakenly thought the first half was about cowboys acting in manly ways, the second half about media people acting in womanly ways. He had been misled by archetypal fantasies about inherently manly and unmanly actions, the same fantasies that impelled him to fistfights and head-butting. Didion perceived that the book was driven by his craftsman's sense of the ways in which women's and men's styles of speech were shaped by social norms and conventions, not eternal archetypes.

II.

Norman Mailer's mother was born in Lithuania shortly before her family emigrated to New Jersey and went into business running hotels for Jewish vacationers. Mailer's father, whose parents had emigrated from Lithuania to South Africa, was born in Johannesburg, moved to Brooklyn as a young man, and met Mailer's mother at her family's hotel. Their son was born in 1923 and grew up first in New Jersey, then in Brooklyn, always in a climate of lies.

His father was a womanizer and a secret compulsive gambler. His mother subtracted ten years from her age and said she was born in America. In the most thorough biography, Michael Lennon's *Norman Mailer: A Double Life* (2013), she is a consistently baleful figure—refusing help for a faked heart attack until her daughter renounced a gentile boyfriend, telling reporters after Mailer stabbed his wife, "My boy's a genius," explaining to another wife that he "needed more love than other men," telling her son that she had prayed while nursing him, "Please God, make him a great man some day," and descending periodically with fresh supplies of narcissism for him to mainline. Mailer said she never left his father because doing so "would interfere with the largest...work of her life, which happened to be me."

Encouraged by her, he wrote a 35,000-word novel when he was eleven, then abandoned writing until he found his vocation when a Harvard English professor assigned Farrell's *Studs Lonigan,* Dos Passos's *U.S.A.,* and Steinbeck's *The Grapes of Wrath.* Shortly after graduating in 1943 he published a story in a commercial anthology, married for the first time, was drafted into the army, and endured the Pacific island battles that he fictionalized in *The Naked and the Dead.*

Everyone reviewed the book as if it belonged to the gritty, realistic tradition of Farrell and Dos Passos, but Mailer said he had been on "a mystic kick" when he wrote it. He told his editor, "There are going to be troubling terrifying glimpses of order in disorder, of a horror which may or may not lurk beneath the surface of things." The characters include the first of many in his work whose evil impulses open them to "primitive glimpses of a structure behind things," who live "on the edge of a deeper knowledge." The book also includes the first of many ordeals in his fiction and his life in which men test themselves by walking along a dangerous, narrow ridge. The one who fails the test in *The Naked and the Dead* is the college-educated, recently married Jewish boy.

Mailer had thought of himself as an atheist, neither proud nor ashamed to be Jewish, but "nauseated" by the Jewish marriage ceremony that his mother demanded after he married his first wife secretly. The glimpses of deep knowledge in *The Naked and the Dead* were not the visionary religious images of his later years, but reflections of Oswald Spengler's determinist history in *The Decline of the*

West, which had the same overpowering effect on Mailer that it has had on many bright, susceptible teenagers.

The Naked and the Dead glanced toward an American future in which centralized control would "masquerade under a conservative liberalism," but the book had little else to say about partisan politics. Mailer, meanwhile, had thrown himself into left-wing politics, speechmaking for Henry Wallace's presidential campaign in 1948, then losing faith in Wallace's Soviet-leaning fellow-traveling. In 1949 Mailer was cheered by the crowd when he stood up to speak at the "Stalinoid" (Dwight Macdonald's word) Waldorf Conference in New York, and booed when he sat down, having said that the Soviet and American sides were both moving toward state capitalism and that there was no future in fighting for either. Afterward, he "felt like a rodent" for publicly renouncing Wallace's Progressive Party, but Macdonald sought him out and praised him. For the rest of his life Mailer remained committed to the anti-Stalinist left.

His next novel, *Barbary Shore* was his first attempt to write about politics as myth. Vast ideological forces are embodied in individual persons in a shabby rooming house, "authority and nihilism stalking one another in the orgiastic hollow of this century," as he described them later. The Soviet Union, never named, is the mythical-sounding "land across the sea." The book was a critical failure, and Mailer, joined by his second wife Adele Morales, began dosing himself with drink and marijuana, partly to find comfort, but, increasingly, in order to push open the doors of perception while, in sober moments, seeking the mythical depths beneath the daily headlines.

Then, in 1955, higher than usual on pot, Mailer had "nothing less than a vision of the universe." He now believed in God, but a God very much at home in Mailer's times, an "embattled existential creature," who "is in danger of dying...who can suffer from a moral corruption." "I believe in it," he insisted. "It's the only thing that makes any sense to me." He still cared nothing about modern Judaism, which seemed a shell emptied of its ancient visionary energies—and he wrote a curious sport of a novel narrated by Jesus, *The Gospel According to the Son* (1997)—but he was excited by medieval Jewish mysticism and wrote essays about the Hasidic tales.

The first fruit of his belief was his theory of the hipster, expounded in his 1957 essay "The White Negro" (published in the otherwise unimaginative pages of *Dissent*, the left-wing anti-Stalinist quarterly edited by Irving Howe), and later in interviews, reviews, and fictions. Today, when "hipster" means a submissive herd-follower attuned to the latest gadgets, it is hard to remember that Mailer, only slightly exaggerating its meaning at the time, popularized an image of the hipster as a lonely knight of the spirit attuned to archetypal currents undetectable by the square, like an exiled Obi-Wan Kenobi sensing a deep disturbance in the Force. The hipster is both a theologian who "conceives of Man's fate being tied up with God's fate" and "a philosophical psychopath" whose drama "is that he seeks love" through an "apocalyptic orgasm" that has much in common with the thrill of mere psychopathic violence. Mailer's imaginative genius always dressed his vaguest fantasies in precise-sounding shape and detail.

The sentence in "The White Negro" that caused the most outrage was one in which Mailer attributed "courage of a sort" to two hoodlums who risked their future by killing a storekeeper. (Readers inferred that the killers were black and the victim Jewish, though Mailer identified neither.) "The hoodlum is therefore daring the unknown, and so no matter how brutal the act it is not altogether cowardly." Mailer, here and elsewhere, made the aesthete's perennial error of confusing the bravery or intensity of an action with its merit. His argument has been defended by citing T. S. Eliot on Baudelaire—"it is better, in a paradoxical way, to do evil than to do nothing"—but an argument is no less muddled because Eliot happened to make it. For the next few decades, against all the evidence of his experience, Mailer still imagined that some extreme *déréglement de tous les sens*, brought about by drugs, drink, or violence, would again reveal the deep instinctive truths promised by his religious ideas. Reality kept knocking him to the mat, but he always sprang up again, punching his way to transcendence.

The nadir of Mailer's quest for intensity occurred in 1960 during a party at which he had planned to announce his mayoral campaign. Drunk and stoned, he spent the evening hitting friends with his fists and other convenient objects. Around four in the morning he got into a shouting match with Adele and stabbed her twice with a penknife, once in the back, once in the chest.

In later years, Mailer explained away the stabbing as an edgy performance that unpredictably went wrong. He only intended, he said, to nick Adele lightly, but accidentally came within a fraction of an inch of her heart. The only other firsthand report, by the victim herself, seems consistent with everything else known about that night. Adele (in her memoir *The Last Party*, 1997) remembers a stranger and her husband standing over her:

"My God, man," he said to Norman, "what have you done? We've got to get her to a hospital."
I felt Norman kick me. "Get away from her, let the bitch die."
Norman grabbed the guy, punching him, as they wrestled all over the room.

Michael Lennon's biography, which portrays Mailer's life mostly as a sequence of disconnected events, describes him as quietly picking himself up and resuming work in the months after the stabbing: "He was mending." Mailer's last wife, Norris Church Mailer, suggests a more plausible and sympathetic version that makes sense of the second half of his career. Mailer, she writes in her memoir *A Ticket to the Circus* (2010), "could pull himself out of the grasp of mental illness by an act of willpower and come back to win Pulitzer Prizes and lead a good life."

Norris Church Mailer is the best guide to another much-reported episode, when Mailer championed the prison writings of Jack Henry Abbott, a murderer who was paroled in 1981 and enjoyed six weeks of celebrity in New York before stabbing to death a waiter who told him that his restaurant had no public restroom. Abbott had not been released on Mailer's recommendation, as news reports suggested, but because, without Mailer's knowledge, Abbott was a stool pigeon who fingered prisoners and lawyers who had organized a work stoppage and, he alleged, dealt drugs. Mailer also knew nothing of Abbott's continuing record of violence or the warnings by prison psychiatrists that he was paranoid and "capable of sudden violence."

Norris makes clear that Mailer, with his mythical imaginings that were far more vivid to him than any psychological insight, was an easy mark for a con man, and was thoroughly manipulated by Abbott's rhetorical skill. Abbott portrayed himself in his letters—published with Mailer's help as *In the Belly of the Beast* (1981)—as, in effect, the true hipster whom Mailer had only imagined, a victim driven to fierce, hardly contained, almost visionary anger by the impersonal state authority that Mailer despised. At the same time that Mailer was praising Abbot's "search for inviolability," Abbot, in circumstances that remain unclear, was colluding with the warden and the United States attorney, reporting real or imaginary misdeeds by lawyers who kept getting in their way. Mailer brought Abbott to New York, and when he murdered in New York, it was no consolation to Mailer that he would likely have murdered somewhere else if Mailer had never heard of him. Mailer never wrote again about psychotic hipsters.

III.

In 1956, desperate to meet a deadline, Mailer wrote a column for the *Village Voice,* a paper he had helped to create, nominating Ernest Hemingway for president of the United States. Like Hemingway, Mailer inspired admiration for a hypermasculine simplified version of himself. Among the intoxicating ideas that Mailer's critics and admirers serve up as two-hundred-proof Mailer, many are in fact bourbon-and-Lawrence. Mailer on the "psychic tendrils" of the womb and its "waves of communication to some conceivable source of life" is an echo of Lawrence's vision of the solar plexus in *Fantasia of the Unconscious.* Mailer's excremental romanticism (the anus as a center of power, feces as "the riches of Satan") copies the "Excurse" chapter in *Women in Love.* Mailer's fantasies about the psychosomatic etiology of cancer derive from Georg Groddeck via Wilhelm Reich. In each instance, Mailer used more words than his sources and said less.

The standard biographical account of Mailer's sex life as a greathearted Don Juan with women waiting in every city—typified by Michael Lennon's account of it—tends toward a leering admiration that inspires skepticism. Norris Church Mailer tells a more plausible story. Both she and Lennon describe the awkward moment when she met Mailer's Chicago girlfriend, but only Norris adds the detail that the woman "was his age if not older; she wore a gray wig, was about five feet tall, and must have weighed two hundred and fifty pounds or more." When Norris asked what had attracted him, Mailer "said that sometimes he needed to be the good-looking one." Norris learned that Mailer's other secret lovers resembled the one in Chicago—Mailer's friends were struck by the erotic edge in his friendship with Diana Trilling, eighteen years his senior—and although

Norris doesn't mention it, the photos of Mailer's mother that she includes in her memoir fit the same description.

Forty years earlier, the narrator of *Barbary Shore* lusted after an "undeniably short and stout" older woman; in bed with a young slender one, he "performed" "without tenderness or desire." Like Lionel Trilling's *The Middle of the Journey*, *Barbary Shore* is a book driven by mixed erotic feelings while presenting itself as a book about politics. Mailer's only sibling was his younger sister; in the florid Oedipal fantasia of *Barbary Shore,* the narrator and the stout older woman are interrupted during foreplay by the woman's young daughter. The book ends when the woman's wretched failure of a husband is shot to death by a government agent, and the narrator, having watched the killing without having had any part in it, flees the house and takes up a new identity as though he had been the guilty one.

In public, Mailer provoked masculine envy by squiring beauties and presented himself as a prophet of sexual energy that broke social constraints. His real sexuality seems to have been the opposite, a lifelong performance by an actor hungry for applause from two audiences—a public one impressed by his books and wives, and the audience in his mind that wanted to see himself as the adored good-looking one.* At thirty he wrote in his journal that his desires were the polymorphous wishes of infancy: "I, whose sexual nature is to cling to one woman like a child embracing the universe, am driven by my destiny to be the orgiast, or at least the intellectual mentor of orgiasm."

---

* His performance seems to have provided vicarious pleasure that was important to much of his audience. After a version of this chapter appeared in *The New York Review of Books*, a half-dozen men wrote to me declaring their admiration for Mailer as (they almost all used the same word) a "cocksman."

Part of his performance as mentor of orgiasm was his theorizing about the hipster's "search for an orgasm more apocalyptic than the one which preceded it." The hipster pursued that orgasm through acts of dominance, but the "extreme contradictions of the society which formed his character" made it "as remote as the Holy Grail." Could the hipster attain apocalyptic orgasm, he would experience a visionary ecstasy of power. Mailer's theories about hipsters ignored all the testimony of literature and life that describes sexually induced visionary experiences, whatever play of dominance leads up to them, as visions of gratitude, equality, and awe.

Mailer knew all this when he wrote about real persons—including himself when he wrote privately in his journal—instead of mythical hipsters. For D.H. Lawrence, "sexual transcendence" was "some ecstasy where he could lose...his sense of self and his will." Lawrence achieved ecstasy through "dominance over women," but because he was physically weak, psychological dominance "was not tyranny to him but equality." Mailer's sense of himself as "the good-looking one" was for him the form of dominance that, by balancing his inner weakness, made equality possible.

Mailer's friends wondered why he encouraged attacks on himself from women outraged by his theories, as he did at Town Hall in 1971 when he moderated a "Dialogue on Women's Liberation" that he knew would be a well-publicized assault. He was performing a role that required a large supporting cast of antagonists; the more that women felt provoked by him, the more masculine he seemed to himself. His provocations had some unwanted effects. Germaine Greer was on the panel with him at Town Hall, unsettling the audience with her clear signals of erotic interest in him. A friend who afterward shared a taxi with both of them reported that Mailer had to flee from the cab to escape being dragged into bed by her. (In her version of the story, she was the reluctant one.)

Mailer always acknowledged in indirect ways that he was the loser in the sexual wars he provoked. "The Time of Her Time" (1959) is the notorious story in which Sergius O'Shaugnessy—a character from *The Deer Park,* now a hipster somehow earning his living as a bullfighting instructor in Greenwich Village—brings a repressed college student to her first orgasm through anal and vaginal sex with the organ that Sergius calls "my avenger." As attentive readers noticed, Sergius finally provokes the girl to orgasm by whispering in her ear, "You dirty little Jew"—psychologically effective but scarcely a triumph of the avenger. At the end the girl proves to be the matador, Sergius the fallen bull:

> I could see the look in her eyes, that unmistakable point for the kill that you find in the eyes of very few bullfighters.... She came on for her moment of truth by saying, "He [Sergius' friend] told me your whole life is a lie, and you do nothing but run away from the homosexual that is you."
>
> And like a real killer, she did not look back, and was out the door before I could rise to tell her that she was a hero fit for me.

In 2007, a few months before he died at eighty-four, Mailer visited his San Francisco lover during a publicity tour. They met in the hotel restaurant and talked about his surgeries. Then he asked, "Would you like to come up to the room?" She declined: "If I come up, I'll fall asleep." He replied that he would too, perhaps still hoping to cling drowsily to a woman "like a child embracing the universe."

7

NEIGHBOR: W. H. AUDEN

I.

W. H. AUDEN'S CHRISTIANITY shaped the tone and content of his poems and was for most of his life the central focus of his art and thought. It was also the aspect of his life and work that seems to have been the least understood by his readers and friends, partly because he sometimes talked about it in frivolous terms, partly because he used Christian vocabulary in ways that, a few centuries earlier, might have attracted the Inquisitor's attention.

T. S. Eliot thought of religion as "the still point in the turning world," "the heart of light," "the crowned knot of fire," "the door we never opened"—something that remained inaccessible, perfect, and eternal, whether or not he or anyone else cared about it, something wholly unlike the sordid transience of human life. Auden thought of religion as derived from the commandment "Thou shalt love thy neighbor as thyself"—an obligation to other human beings despite all their imperfections and his own, and an obligation to the inescapable reality of this world, not a visionary, inaccessible world that might or might not exist somewhere else.

His version of Christianity was more or less incomprehensible to anyone who thought religion was a matter of supernatural beliefs, ancestral identities, moral prohibitions, doctrinal orthodoxies, hierarchical organizations, sectarian arguments, religious emotions, spiritual aspirations, scriptural authority, or any other conventional aspect of personal or organized religion. He insisted that only adults can make a religious commitment, that the imposition of religion on children and adolescents was absurd. He had no interest in the megalomaniac sentimentality embodied by what he called the "Creeping Jesus" in Dostoyevsky's later writings, where the Russian people's love of Christ becomes an ecstatically satisfying excuse for military conquest. Auden also dismissed the popular notion of hell and damnation as "morally revolting and intellectually incredible because it is conceived of in terms of human criminal law, as a torture imposed upon the sinner against his will by an all-powerful God." Many twentieth-century defenses of religion by philosophers and others made much of an irreducible sense of mystery that religion responds to with feelings of awe. Auden thought such feelings were a distraction from religion.

At fifteen, Auden lost the Anglican faith he had learned from his parents. He found it again, in a very different form, at thirty-three, a year after he left his native England to settle in New York. Unlike the ritualized, quasi-magical religion of his childhood, his adult religion was a product of his deracinated life in America, at first deeply interior and intellectualized. He took seriously his membership in the Anglican Church—he took communion every Sunday—and derived many of his moral and aesthetic ideas from Christian doctrines developed over two millennia, but he came to value his church and its doctrines only to the extent that they helped to make it possible to love one's neighbor as oneself. To the extent that they became ends in themselves, or made it easier for a believer to isolate or elevate himself, they became—in the word Auden used about most aspects of institutional Christendom—unchristian. Church doctrines, like all human creations, were subject to judgment.

He made a point of acknowledging that any belief he might have in a monotheist personal God was a product of the anthropomorphic language in which human beings think. Late in life, after reading a *Scientific American* article about the microbes living on the human skin, he wrote a poem that asked what religious beliefs such creatures might devise—by projecting from their circumstances—in the hope of making moral sense of their world:

> If you were religious folk,
> how would your dramas justify
> unmerited suffering?

> By what myths would your priests account
> for the hurricanes that come
> twice every twenty-four hours,
> each time I dress or undress,
> when, clinging to keratin rafts,
> whole cities are swept away
> to perish in space, or the Flood
> that scalds to death when I bathe?

All religious statements about God, he thought, must be false in a literal sense but might be true in metaphoric ones. He felt himself commanded by an absolute obligation—which he knew he could never fulfill—to love his neighbor as himself. A haiku he wrote late in life seems to allude to the moment when he first experienced that command in a personal way: "He has never seen God / but, once or twice, he believes / he has heard Him."*

"To pray," Auden wrote, "is to pay attention or, shall we say, to 'listen' to someone or something other than oneself. Whenever a man so concentrates his attention—be it on a landscape, or a poem or a geometrical problem or an idol or the True God—that he completely forgets his own ego and desires in listening to what the other has to say to him, he is praying." To more conventional beliefs this seems a denatured idea of prayer, but Auden took it seriously, and seems to have prayed in exactly this sense. The only value he found in "petitionary prayer"—prayer that asks for something—was that the act of expressing desires can reveal unwelcome truths about what they are, so that "we often discover that they are really wishes that two-and-two should make three or five, as when St. Augustine realized that he was praying: 'Lord, make me chaste, but not yet.'" Auden prayed to a God whom he knew he thought about in falsely human-centered terms, but that was the only way he could listen with any attention: "I can see...what leads [Paul] Tillich, for example, to speak of God as the 'Ground of Being,' but if I try to pray: 'O Thou Ground, have mercy upon me,' I start to giggle."

Auden imagined judging a critic's taste by asking if the critic liked—"and by like I really mean like, not approve of on principle"— among other things "long lists of proper names such as the Old Testament genealogies or the Catalogue of ships in the *Iliad*." His poems displayed his own passion for proper names, for example the list of "names on my numinous map" pointed to places personally sacred to him, his inward map

---

* "Once or twice": in a lecture he wrote around the same time as this haiku he alluded to another command that he heard when he chose to be a poet: "I know the most convinced atheist scientist has prayed at least once in his life, when he heard a voice say, 'Thou shalt serve Science.'"

of the *Solihull* gas-works, gazed at in awe
by a bronchial boy, the *Blue John Mine,*
the *Festiniog* railway, the *Rhyader* dams,
Cross Fell, Keld and *Cauldron Snout,*

of sites made sacred by something read there,
a lunch, a good lay, or sheer lightness of heart,
the *Fürbringer* and the *Friedrich Strasse,*
Isafjördur, Epomeo,
Poprad, Basel, Bar-le-Duc,

of more modern holies, *Middagh Street,*
Carnegie Hall, and the *Con-Ed* stacks
on *First Avenue...**

His pleasure in names had a moral and theological point. Like
prayer, it was a form of attention. Every proper name was a sign of
personal uniqueness, and this was true no matter how common the
name might be—John or Mary do not think of themselves as members of a tribe of people who share the same first name—and Auden
used the word "miracle" to refer to anyone's sense of the unique value
of one's own unpredictable individuality. "To give someone or something a Proper Name," he wrote, "is to acknowledge it as having a
real and valuable existence, independent of its use to oneself, in other
words, to acknowledge it as a neighbor." The value that is acknowledged through a proper name is not measurable in any objective
sense; it exists in the eyes of the beholder. When human beings imagine a beholder who finds such value everywhere, they think in terms
of God, or, as Auden wrote in another late poem, "the One... / Who

---

* The last of these refers to the smokestacks on a Manhattan power plant.

numbers each particle / by its Proper Name"—a deity who knows the personal name of every electron in the universe, rather than thinking about them in collective, statistical terms.[*]

Auden referred to himself as a "would-be Christian," because, he said, even to call oneself a Christian would be an unchristian act of pride. "Christianity is a way, not a state, and a Christian is never something one is, only something one can pray to become." To become a Christian, as he understood it, did not require belief in an immortal soul separable from the body (he called this a Platonic, not a Christian, doctrine) nor in the resurrection of Christ (which he only mentioned in order to remark that he could not make himself believe in it) nor in miracles that violated the laws of physics.

II.

Both science and religion were at the heart of Auden's family culture. His father was a physician, medical researcher, and amateur archaeologist who became professor of public health at Birmingham University and Birmingham's first school medical officer; he seems to have been the first public official in Britain to use psychoanalytic methods, and published essays on many classical and modern subjects, including the first medical account of autoerotic strangulation.

---

[*] From his poem "Epithalamium (for Peter Mudford and Rita Auden, May 15th, 1965)." This updates Psalm 147: "He telleth the number of the stars; he calleth them all by their names." The other power the poem attributes to this hypothetical deity is the ability to see relations invisible to human beings between disparate things: he is the "One for whom / all enantiomorphs are superposable" (enantiomorphs are mirror-image three-dimensional shapes, such as a pair of gloves, that can be made to coincide point for point, i.e., superposed, only in four-dimensional space).

Auden's mother trained as a nurse after earning an honors degree from London University. Auden, who was born in 1907, impressed his schoolmates with arcane sexual and psychoanalytic knowledge gleaned from his father's library.

The family was Anglo-Catholic, the name given to members of the most ritualistic and least Protestant wing of the Church of England. As a child, Auden experienced religion as a mysterious and exciting ritual in which he performed the role of boat-boy, the child who carries the incense for the priest to cast over the congregation, and at thirteen he went through a "period of ecclesiastical *Schwärmerei*," an episode of religious enthusiasm that he later understood as an emotional response to puberty.

In 1922, when Auden was fifteen, one of his school friends was embarrassed by learning in a casual conversation that Auden was religious, and changed the subject by asking whether he wrote poetry. He had never done so, but, as he recalled later in a poem, he suddenly discovered his vocation: "I knew / That very moment what I wished to do." He later recorded 1922 as the year in which he "discovers that he has lost his faith." For the adolescent Auden, poetry provided the magical excitement that he had earlier found in religion.

During the next fifteen years he explained the world to his friends and himself in terms of psychology and economics, which he more or less explicitly thought of as the triumphant successors to religion. He built—and continuously rebuilt—an intellectual framework out of a jumbled storehouse of ideas derived from Freud, D. H. Lawrence, Marx, and a dozen lesser-known figures who served as temporary heroes, such as the Jungian anthropologist John Layard and the mystical polymath Gerald Heard.

As an undergraduate at Oxford in the 1920s he had no politics and never read a newspaper. A year in Berlin in 1928–29, where Nazis and Communists were battling in the streets, gave him the sense of a world starting to crumble. His first book, *Poems,* published in 1930 when he was twenty-three, and his second, *The Orators,* two years later, made him famous as the literary voice of a new generation's private and public anxieties. At the depth of the Depression, around 1932, he wrote a few poems in the voice of a working-class revolutionary who did not hold Auden's own views ("I am a bourgeois," Auden wrote to a friend, "I shall not join the C[ommunist] P[arty]") but who gave unambivalent assent to political attitudes that Auden himself held only with mixed feelings:

> Comrades who when the sirens roar
> From office shop and factory pour
>   'Neath evening sky;
> By cops directed to the fug
> Of talkie-houses* for a drug
> Or down canals to find a hug
>   Until you die...

These poems, and Auden's politically-tinged early plays, called for the destruction of the comfortable, civilized life he had grown up in, but—like much revolutionary literature before and since—they were also instruments of private ambition, giving him the status of literary hero to the English left.

Meanwhile, though he thought he had finished with Christianity forever, he was still using a Christian vocabulary. Christopher Isherwood, who collaborated with him on three plays, wrote at the time about his reliance on the tone and form of the liturgy:

---

* "The fug of talkie-houses" means the stuffy air in cinemas showing sound films, introduced to Britain in 1929.

When we collaborate, I have to keep a sharp eye on him—or down flop the characters on their knees. . . . If Auden had his way, he would turn every play into a cross between grand opera and high mass.

His apparently secular poems often had a hidden religious starting-point. An ominous ballad he wrote in 1932 seems to be set in eighteenth-century England with its "scarlet soldiers":

> O what is that sound which so thrills the ear
>> Down in the valley, drumming, drumming?
> Only the scarlet soldiers, dear,
>> The soldiers coming.

The poem ends in a disastrous betrayal of love and trust:

> O where are you going? stay with me here!
>> Were the vows you swore me deceiving, deceiving?
> No, I promised to love you, dear,
>> But I must be leaving.
>
> O it's broken the lock and splintered the door,
>> O it's the gate where they're turning, turning;
> Their feet are heavy on the floor
>> And their eyes are burning.

But as Auden recalled later, the stimulus for the poem was a painting of the Agony in the Garden, where the soldiers in the background appear harmless, and "it is only because one has read the Gospel story, that one knows that, in fact, they are coming to arrest Jesus." The poem's image of erotic betrayal has invisible links to other kinds of betrayal.

The first step in Auden's return to the church seems to have begun in 1933 with an experience that he later described as "not overtly Christian," although the memory of it, he said, was "one of the most crucial" factors that helped to bring him back to the Anglican Church seven years later. He called it a "vision of Agape," that is, of shared unerotic love. The place was the Downs School, in the west of England, where Auden was a teacher:

> One fine summer night in June 1933 I was sitting on a lawn after dinner with three colleagues, two women and one man. We liked each other well enough but we were certainly not intimate friends, nor had any one of us a sexual interest in another. Incidentally, we had not drunk any alcohol. We were talking casually about everyday matters when, quite suddenly and unexpectedly, something happened. I felt myself invaded by a power which, though I consented to it, was irresistible and certainly not mine. For the first time in my life I knew exactly— because, thanks to the power, I was doing it—what it means to love one's neighbor as oneself.... My personal feelings towards them were unchanged—they were still colleagues, not intimate friends—but I felt their existence as themselves to be of infinite value and rejoiced in it.

The poem he wrote at the time about this experience, "A Summer Night," is exuberantly grateful for it without quite saying what it was—the poem calls it "this for which we dread to lose / Our privacy" or simply "it"—and ends by hoping that "it" might reemerge after an impending social revolution, as a force bringing forgiveness and calm.

Neither this nor any later religious experience gave him self-satisfaction. His poem looks forward without regret to a revolution that will destroy himself and his class. He wrote in his later recollection that he knew, at the time, that the experience would end sooner or later, and that, "when it did, my greeds and self-regard would return....The memory of the experience has not prevented me from making use of others...but it has made it much more difficult for me to deceive myself about what I am up to when I do." The same idea was behind a statement he once made that the purpose of art, to the extent that it has one, is to make self-deception more difficult, and, "by telling the truth, to disenchant and disintoxicate."

The Nazis' rise to power in that same year, 1933, made large moral questions seem suddenly more urgent. "The novelty and shock of the Nazis," he wrote later, "was that they made no pretense of believing in justice and liberty for all, and attacked Christianity on the grounds that to love one's neighbor as oneself was a command fit only for effeminate weaklings." Moreover, he continued,

> this utter denial of everything liberalism had ever stood for was arousing wild enthusiasm, not in some remote barbaric land outside the pale, but in one of the most highly educated countries in Europe....Confronted by such a phenomenon, it was impossible any longer to believe that the values of liberal humanism were self-evident. Unless one was prepared to take a relativist view that all values are a matter of personal taste, one could hardly avoid asking the question: "If, as I am convinced, the Nazis are wrong and we are right, what is it that validates our values and invalidates theirs?"

Communism opposed Nazism but offered no answer to this question. The Communists, Auden wrote, promised to create a future world in which everyone would love their neighbors, but they claimed that in order to do so, "one must hate and destroy some of one's neighbors now."

At school and university, Auden's intellectual confidence had given him power and authority among his friends. When his Oxford tutor challenged his students to justify an outlandish literary or scholarly judgment, they sometimes answered, "That's what Wystan says." Now, in 1933, he began to imagine he could combine his father's powers as a healer and his own poetic powers to undo the psychological and moral failures of his neighbors and nation. He wrote two expansive, ambitious poems, each urging someone unnamed to write words that will cure and transform those who read. The first, from 1933, begins, "Friend, of the civil space by human love," and urges the "Friend" to "sit down and write":

So write that reading is changing in their living, these
May save in time their generation and their race...

The second, from early in 1934, begins "'Sweet is it,' say the doomed, 'to be alive though wretched,'" and addresses a potential "pioneer":

So do, so speak, so write that each upon
This mortal star may feel himself the danger
That under his hand is softly palpitating.

"Quieten that hand," he urges. "O reconcile."

The healer-pioneer he had in mind, the one writer who combined all the many concerns spelled out in these poems, was himself, though he was also remembering two earlier examples, both now dead. He wrote a review (also early in 1934) citing Lenin and T. E. Lawrence ("Lawrence of Arabia") as "potent agents of freedom...the most relevant accusation and hope."

This heady messianic fantasy seem to have been Auden's means of escape from his deep, persistent, but always unspecific sense of guilt—what he called in one of these poems "that guilt which prisons every upright person." Like all anxious guilt, it had no single cause, no clear etiology. It focused at times on his class privileges, at times on his homosexuality, which he seems to have thought of, at the time, as "crooked," or inherently criminal, unlike the sexuality that was "straight."

He recoiled guiltily from this fantasy almost as soon as he expressed it. (Intermittently throughout his life, whenever he wanted to rid himself of something deep in his psyche, he first gave it a voice in his poems.) He discarded both of his messianic poems before he could publish them.* A few weeks after writing the second one, he wrote two sonnets dismissing his fantasy as a psychological and moral failure of his own. Both sonnets used his lifelong technique of describing himself in the third person. In one (which he never published) he wrote: "To him the wretched are a race apart, / He is not yet their indifferent redeemer." In the other, "Just as his dream foretold," he imagined himself arriving at a welcoming house where "the talk always took the wished-for turn, / Dwelt on the need for stroking and advice," though he could not evade the question of who it was who needed to be rescued by medicine, love, or revolution:

Which was in need of help? Were they or he
The physician, bridegroom and incendiary?

Two years later, in *The Ascent of F6,* one of the plays he wrote in collaboration with Isherwood, he portrayed a lightly-disguised Lawrence of Arabia as the self-destructive megalomaniac climber Michael Ransom. To dramatize Ransom's ranting messianic fantasy, he

---

* He recited the second one in a BBC broadcast, and submitted it to T. S. Eliot's quarterly *The Criterion,* but then he either withdrew it or Eliot rejected it.

put into his mouth two dozen lines from the poems he had abandoned after writing them in 1934. As for his idea of Lenin as an agent of freedom, Auden began revising his earlier poems to remove any positive words about communism.

Then the Spanish Civil War erupted in 1936, and Auden again felt he must take political action, but now in a way that had nothing to do with his intellect or art. In 1937, before he was thirty, he was famous enough for the London *Daily Worker* to print on its front page the news that he had left for Spain, intending to drive an ambulance for the beleaguered socialist Republic against the invading fascists. When he got there, the government instead put him to work broadcasting propaganda, a job he gave up after about a week.

After visiting the front, and discovering for himself the moral ambiguities and failures of his own side that George Orwell later reported in *Homage to Catalonia,* he quietly left. Back in England, he wrote his poem "Spain" in support of the Republic, a public oration that said nothing about his feelings:

Tomorrow for the young the poets exploding like bombs,
The walks by the lake, the weeks of perfect communion;
    Tomorrow the bicycle races
Through the suburbs on summer evenings. But today the struggle.

For many years he was uncharacteristically silent in public about what he had seen in Spain. He wrote about it only once, almost twenty years afterward, in an essay on his return to the church:

On arriving in Barcelona, I found as I walked through the city that all the churches were closed and there was not a priest to be seen. To my astonishment, this discovery left me profoundly shocked and disturbed. The feeling was far too intense to be the result of a mere liberal dislike of intolerance, the notion that it is wrong to stop people from doing what they like, even if it is something silly like going to church. I could not escape acknowledging that, however I had consciously ignored and rejected the Church for sixteen years, the existence of churches and what went on in them had all the time been very important to me.

In 1937, a few months after he got back from Spain, he met the writer and publisher Charles Williams.* For the first time in his life, he said later, he felt himself "in the presence of personal sanctity." As in 1933 when he found himself loving his neighbors for themselves, now, although he and Williams talked only business, he "felt transformed into a person who was incapable of doing or thinking anything base or unloving."

The moral language of Christianity now became more and more explicit in his work. He wrote an essay on the conflicts between the rational, conscious side of the mind and the instinctual, unconscious side, and ended with the speculation: "Perhaps...the only thing that can bring them together is the exercise of what Christians call Charity." He wrote a ballad, "As I walked out one evening," in which a lover proclaims in clichés his perfect, faithful love:

"I'll love you, dear, I'll love you
    Till China and Africa meet,
And the river jumps over the mountain
    And the salmon sing in the street."

---

* He visited Williams, who worked at the Oxford University Press, to propose that he compile an *Oxford Book of Light Verse*, a book of popular, not coterie, poetry from the middle ages to the present, "having for its subject-matter the everyday social life of its period or the experiences of the poet as an ordinary human being." Auden's anthology, which appeared in 1938, was a non-partisan, non-propagandistic vehicle for his populist views.

Then "all the clocks in the city" chime out the inescapable reality of mortality and imperfection: "Time watches from the shadow / And coughs when you would kiss." The clocks end with a command:

> "O stand, stand at the window
>   As the tears scald and start;
> You shall love your crooked neighbor
>   With your crooked heart."

This does not contradict the biblical commandment, but restates it in terms suitable to the flawed reality of human beings.

A few weeks later, he wrote "Musée des Beaux Arts," a commentary on Brueghel's *Landscape with the Fall of Icarus* (1558, in the collection of the Musées Royeaux des Beaux-Arts in Brussels) and the indifference with which everyone in the painting registers Icarus's death:

> About suffering they were never wrong,
> The Old Masters: how well they understood
> Its human position; how it takes place
> While someone else is eating or opening a window or just walking dully along...

> In Brueghel's *Icarus*, for instance: how everything turns away
> Quite leisurely from the disaster; the ploughman may
> Have heard the splash, the forsaken cry,
> But for him it was not an important failure...
> ...and the expensive delicate ship that must have seen
> Something amazing, a boy falling out of the sky,
> Had somewhere to get to and sailed calmly on.

The poem also sketches the outline of the Christian story: it mentions, as if in passing, a "miraculous birth," a "dreadful martyrdom," and Icarus' "forsaken cry"—an echo of the victim in the gospels who "cried with a loud voice, 'My God, my God, why hast thou forsaken me?'"

No one could have helped Icarus, and the poem condemns no one. Everyone has "somewhere to get to." But its moral point—one that Auden addressed mostly to himself, and that hardens into sanctimony as soon as it is stated rather than implied—is that human indifference, no matter how commonplace, is a moral failure, a refusal to love one's neighbor. And that commonplace failure has universal significance. As Auden noted, the gospels describe the commandments to love one's God and to love one's neighbor as "like" each other, and for Auden the moral significance of one's neighbor becomes clear when one thinks of him as created in the image of God.

III.

In January 1939 Auden left England for America, partly in the hope of escaping his own public status. Instead he arrived as a conqueror. Long after he and a group of American poets read their poems at a public meeting in New York, to an audience of about a thousand, William Carlos Williams still bitterly recalled in his diary that "Auden's success before the audience as contrasted with the rest of us [the Americans] was the feature of the evening."

His messianic fantasy resurfaced when W. B. Yeats died three days after Auden arrived in New York, and Auden became the most prominent living British-born poet. His poem "In Memory of W. B. Yeats" ends with another of his addresses to himself. Yeats has been "laid to rest," and the poem tells an unnamed living poet to follow him to the realms of death, but to reemerge, as Yeats no longer can, to teach and to heal:

Follow poet, follow right
To the bottom of the night,
With your unconstraining voice
Still persuade us to rejoice;

With the farming of a verse
Make a vineyard of the curse,
Sing of human unsuccess
In a rapture of distress;

In the deserts of the heart
Let the healing fountain start,
In the prison of his days
Teach the free man how to praise.

New York transformed Auden's sense of himself. Three months after he arrived he met and fell in love with Chester Kallman, a eighteen-year-old poet and Brooklyn College student whose extrovert Jewish wit was the antithesis of his English reserve. They began a relationship that Auden thought of as a marriage; he, not Kallman, wore a ring. Writing a few months later about Verlaine and Rimbaud, he referred offhandedly to "their marriage." He wrote a poem, "In Sickness and in Health," that celebrated, with no gendered pronouns, his relation with Kallman. His guilty sense of his homosexuality had been supplanted by his growing sense that the only serious moral questions were concerned with loving one's neighbor as oneself, that specific varieties of sexuality were irrelevant to such matters. He wrote to a friend in England: "*America:* The most decisive experience of my life so far.... For the first time I am leading a life which remotely approximates to the way I think I ought to live."

Privately, he was still arguing against himself, and guiltily recoiling from his own success. Six months after he arrived in New York, after making a speech at a political meeting, he wrote to a friend:

> I suddenly found I could really do it, that I could make a fighting demagogic speech and have the audience roaring.... It is so exciting but so absolutely degrading; I felt just covered with dirt afterwards.

When war broke out in September 1939, he tried to console himself with a new fantasy about historical inevitability, a new belief that everyone's divided self would someday find inner peace and harmony with everyone else. He told himself and his friends that a just and loving society would emerge inevitably, that the horror of Nazism was a disastrous but temporary detour on the road to a secular New Jerusalem. When he drafted his poem "September 1, 1939," he included a stanza "To testify my faith" that all human error "can / Delay but cannot prevent / The education of man."

This stanza answered his question of what validated his values and refuted the Nazis' by stating his belief that the universe was on his side, not theirs. Sooner or later, everyone would be forced by evolution, by history, into loving their neighbor whether they now wanted to or not. Auden later realized that this idea makes nonsense of the commandment to love one's neighbor, because a commandment assumes that everyone is free to refuse it; no one needs to hear a commandment before deciding to breathe or sleep. Auden crossed out this stanza before sending off the poem.* A few years later, when he put together the first collected edition of his work, he dropped another stanza, the one that contained his most famous line, "We must love one another or die," because, by treating love as a physical necessity like breathing rather than as a matter of personal choice, it affirmed the same nonsense. In public he gave a simpler explanation for dropping the line—"We must die anyway"—but what he despised about it was its empty meliorist piety. Fifteen years later he ended a poem about a rainstorm: "Thousands have lived without love, not one without water."

Even at the time, he seems to been hoping half-consciously for some moral or intellectual shock to dislodge his fantasy of inevitable universal love. He found it in November 1939 when he went to a German-language cinema in Manhattan which was showing a German newsreel celebrating the Nazi victory over Poland. (Until the United States and Germany declared war, German films could be shown freely in American theaters.) Auden was startled by the shouts of "Kill the Poles!" that rose from the audience of ordinary German immigrants who were under no coercion to support the Nazis. He told an interviewer many years later: "I wondered, then, why I reacted as I did against this denial of every humanistic value. The answer brought me back to the church."

A few weeks later, in 1940, he began attending Sunday services ("in a tentative and experimental sort of way") near his flat in Brooklyn Heights, and began reading Søren Kierkegaard, Paul Tillich, and other Protestant theologians whose theology emphasized moral absolutes and who tended to ignore supernatural beliefs as vestiges of

---

* More precisely, this stanza was still in his typescript when he submitted it to *The New Yorker*, which turned it down as unsuitable for magazine's tone. He then crossed out the stanza (and another one on the same theme) and sent the typescript to *The New Republic*, which accepted it.

older folk religions. After about ten months, he began taking communion and, by doing so, formally returned to the Anglican church, though still divided—as he would be always—between faith and doubt. The book he wrote during these ten months was titled *The Double Man.* It had an epigraph from Montaigne: "We are, I know not how, double in ourselves, so that what we believe we disbelieve, and cannot rid ourselves of what we condemn."

He seems to have said nothing to his friends about his return to the church. When he wrote to T. S. Eliot—his editor and publisher in Britain—that "thanks to Charles Williams and Kierkegaard I have come to pretty much the same position as yourself, which I was brought up in anyway," he added in parentheses, "Please don't tell anyone this." At the same time, he was keeping his views hidden from his readers by filling his prose with pompous, polysyllabic exhortations about the need for "absolute presuppositions" and a "metaphysics" that can give a culture its intellectual framework, and his vocabulary pointed toward an impersonal philosophical view, not the inwardly religious one that he had in fact adopted.

The motives for his reticence can only be guessed at. Part may have been embarrassment at having arrived at an intellectually unfashionable view that contradicted the Freudian and Marxist doctrines for which he had been lionized. Part may have been his embarrassment at having once preached political doctrines without fully believing them. Then, in 1941, he began to expound his views in a remote and schoolmasterly way by reviewing books that stated similar views, such as Reinhold Niebuhr's *The Nature and Destiny of Man* and Denis de Rougemont's *Love in the Western World.* He concluded his review of de Rougemont:

In the last few chapters of his book Mr. de Rougemont states the Christian doctrine of marriage, which will seem absurdly straitlaced to the hedonist and shockingly coarse to the romantic. But perhaps the unpleasant consequences of romantic love and romantic politics [Auden's shorthand for fascism] are making thoughtful people more willing to reconsider it than they were while a bourgeois convention [i.e., bourgeois marriage], which professed to be Christian but was nothing of the kind, was still *à la mode*.

A few weeks after Auden wrote this implicit praise of his marriage with Kallman, the marriage ended. Kallman broke off their sexual relations because he could not endure Auden's wish for mutual faithfulness. Auden reacted with murderous rage, probably toward Kallman, possibly toward the man with whom Kallman had been unfaithful. A few months later, he wrote in a verse letter to Kallman, "on account of you, I have been, in intention, and almost in act, a murderer." In print, he alluded to this crisis only once, in his essay about his return to the Church:

And then, providentially—for the occupational disease of poets is frivolity—I was forced to know in person what it is like to feel oneself the prey of demonic powers, in both the Greek and the Christian sense, stripped of self-control and self-respect, behaving like a ham actor in a Strindberg play.

The crisis affected his style along with everything else, knocking the pompous metaphysics out of his prose and replacing it with an aphoristic sharpness that included himself among its targets. In 1943 he wrote an exposition of his theology with a title, "Purely Subjective," that disclaimed objective, philosophical authority. He raised the question of what answer a "man who professes himself a Christian" could give if asked, "Why Jesus and not Socrates or Buddha or Confucius or Mohammed?" The only plausible answer he could imagine was: "None of the others arouse all sides of my being to cry 'Crucify Him.'" This was the farthest possible distance from the magical excitement he had found in religion as a child. In later years he made a point of quoting Georg Christoph Lichtenberg: "There is a great difference between still believing something and believing it again." All his beliefs were beliefs again.

IV.

By the time T. S. Eliot accepted Auden's first book of poems in 1930— he was editorial director of at Faber & Faber and editor of the magisterial quarterly *The Criterion*—Eliot had attained the status of something like a literary demigod. His radically modern poetry, combined with his austerely magisterial prose, gave him unique, unchallengeable authority. Lionel Trilling consciously followed Eliot's model when he consolidated his own eminence twenty years later.

Auden was nineteen years younger than Eliot, and he also began his career by modeling himself on Eliot, though with a deliberate young-rebel's adherence to left-wing radicalism instead of Eliot's theologically tinged conservatism. Auden always wrote about Eliot in a tone of reverence and honor, but after he settled in New York his reverent tone masked a deep skepticism about Eliot's authority and beliefs.

In 1940 Auden had written as a repentant prodigal when he told Eliot that he had come to something close to Eliot's religious position. He soon realized that this was true only in the sense that they both attended Christian churches and practiced Anglican ritual. A few years later, with the greatest possible courtesy, he pointed out "a discordant snobbish note" in Eliot's writings on religion and culture, an over-valuing of aristocratic status:

> Mr. Eliot is only partly right, I think, in asserting that in the past the role of transmission [of culture] was played by a class or by classes. For many centuries, it was transmitted by the Church, i.e., by an institution with a hereditary status whose members could be drawn from any social class.

As for the religious allegory in Eliot's late plays, Auden politely insisted he was "absolutely certain" that Eliot never meant to suggest that the characters who were called to a religious vocation had been called because they were more intelligent and from a higher social class than those who were not called, "but that is exactly what the comedy convention he is using is bound to suggest." Eliot's literary eminence, Auden kept suggesting, had tempted him to identify with other kinds of social and political eminence, to treat himself, and invite others to treat him, as one of a superior class of persons.

"Nothing can be essentially serious for man," Auden wrote, "except that which is given to all men alike, and that which is commanded to all men alike." (He elsewhere wrote: "One thing, and one thing only, is serious: loving one's neighbor as one's self.") What he did not quite say publicly about Eliot's religion was that he regarded it as frivolous, not serious, because, as Auden perceived it, it was given and commanded to some superior people and not to everyone else.

What Auden saw in Eliot was a tendency he was also sharply conscious of in himself: the wish to believe in a god who was "an image of his image of himself" (the phrase is from his poem "Terce"). Auden's favorite illustration of this flattering fantasy was the female impersonator Bert Savoy, who was projecting his own image when he remarked in a thunderstorm, "There's Miss God at it again." (The remark was immortalized because Savoy was struck dead by lightning a few moments later.) Among friends, Auden used "Miss God" to refer to his own fantasy of a providential deity, as in: "Miss God has decided to keep me celibate this summer." The joke made a serious point about everyone's wish for a universe whose purposes were adjusted to their own.

After his marriage to Kallman ended in 1941, Auden again felt guilty doubts about his sexuality. He told a friend in 1947 that he had "come to the conclusion that it's wrong to be queer, but that's a long story." What he seems to have had in mind was something he explained in print many years later: "all 'abnormal' sex-acts are rites of symbolic magic" in which the partners do not value each other as themselves but as symbolic stand-ins for someone else, "Son-and/or-Mother" or "Wife-and/or-Husband." Surprisingly for someone as steeped as he was in Freud, Auden underestimated the degree to which heterosexual acts are also rites of symbolic magic, and the terms in which he was judging his sexuality were ones that could apply to any relation.

With nonreligious friends, he remarked that homosexuality was a sin that he intended to persist in. But among theologically minded friends who distinguished Church doctrine from the heart of a religion, he took a different approach. When he told a Russian Orthodox friend about his attempt in the late 1940s to have a relation with a woman (she was Rhoda Jaffee, the model for Rosetta in *The Age of Anxiety*), he said: "It was a sin." (He said the same thing to a secular-minded woman friend whose sympathies he trusted.) For a homosexual, a heterosexual relation was sinful because it was inherently unequal; he could not love a woman with the same degree of bodily love that she could offer him. As he wrote in a poem, "If equal affection cannot be / Let the more loving one be me." He ended a love poem to Rhoda Jaffee, "On and on and on," with a wish to be a neighbor both erotically (with "embodied love") and theologically:

So my embodied love
Which, like most feeling, is
Half humbug and half true,
Asks neighborhood of you.

By the time he wrote this, in 1947, he had grown dissatisfied with the severely inward-looking Protestantism he adopted a few years earlier. He was now thinking about religion in its shared and collective aspects—in terms of the "sacred importance of the body," of the social relations and public obligations of those who belong to a church—and he seems at least to have considered the possibility of converting either to Roman Catholicism or to Judaism. (He once wondered aloud why the only people he enjoyed talking to in New York were Jews.)

In the 1950s and 1960s Auden's religious views began to coincide with those of Dietrich Bonhoeffer, whose letters from the Nazi prison where he was eventually murdered had expounded an adult, "religionless" Christianity that had left behind all childish fantasies of a protective, paternal God. Bonhoeffer's God experienced human suffering: "It is not some religious act which makes a Christian what he is, but participation in the suffering of God in the life of the world."

Auden told friends that of all the doctrines that the early Church had condemned as heresies (such as the Gnostic and Manichaean heresies that regarded matter as inherently fallen or demonic), the only one in which he believed was patripassianism, the doctrine that the Father voluntarily suffered with the Son. He was affirming a heresy in which, as he wrote in "The Shield of Achilles," "one could weep because another wept."

V.

Auden had a secret life that his closest friends knew little or nothing about. Everything about it was generous and honorable. He kept it secret because he would have been ashamed to have been praised for it.

It seems to have begun in his early years in America, but I learned about it mostly by chance, so it may have been far more extensive than I or anyone ever knew. Once at a party I met a woman who attended St. Mark's in-the-Bowery with him in the 1950s. She told me that Auden heard that an old woman in the congregation was suffering night terrors, so he took a blanket and slept in the hallway outside her apartment until she felt safe again.

Someone else recalled that Auden had once been told that a friend needed a medical operation that he couldn't afford. Auden invited the friend to dinner, never mentioned the operation, but as the friend was leaving said, "I want you to have this," and handed him a large notebook containing the manuscript of *The Age of Anxiety*. The University of Texas bought the notebook and the friend had the operation.

From some letters I found in Auden's papers, I learned that shortly after World War II he had arranged through a European relief agency to pay the annual school and college costs for two German war orphans chosen by the agency. His gift remained anonymous until the orphans insisted, after they graduated, on learning his name. When they went to Austria to thank him, he was too embarrassed to say more than a few muttered words.

At times he went out of his way to seem selfish while doing

something selfless. When NBC Television was producing a broadcast of *The Magic Flute* for which he and Kallman had translated the libretto, he stormed into the producer's office demanding to be paid immediately, instead of on the date specified in his contract. He waited there, making himself unpleasant, until a check finally arrived. A few weeks later, when the canceled check came back to NBC, someone noticed that he had endorsed it, "Pay to the order of Dorothy Day." The New York City Fire Department had recently ordered Day to make costly repairs to the homeless shelter she managed for the Catholic Worker Movement, and the shelter would have been shut down had she failed to come up with the money.

At literary gatherings he made a practice of slipping away from "the gaunt and great, the famed for conversation" (as he called them in a poem) to find the least important person in the room. A letter-writer in the *Times* of London reported her memory of one such incident:

Sixty years ago [in 1953] my English teacher brought me to London from my provincial grammar school for a literary conference. Understandably, she abandoned me for her friends when we arrived, and I was left to flounder. I was gauche and inept and had no idea what to do with myself. Auden must have sensed this because he approached me and said, "Everyone here is just as nervous as you are, but they are bluffing, and you must learn to bluff too." His sensitivity and empathy left an indelible impression on me.

Late in life Auden wrote self-revealing poems and essays that portrayed him as insular and nostalgic, still living imaginatively in the Edwardian English world of his childhood. His "Doggerel by a Senior Citizen" began, "Our earth in 1969 / Is not the planet I call mine," and continued with disgruntled complaints against the modern age: "I cannot settle which is worse, / The Anti-Novel or Free Verse." A year after he wrote this declaration of traditionalist provincialism, I chanced on a first book by a young poet, N. J. Loftis, *Exiles and Voyages*. Some of the book was in free verse; much of it alluded to Harlem and Africa. The book was dedicated "To my first friend, W. H. Auden."

A few years later I got a phone call from a Canadian burglar who told me he had come across Auden's poems in a prison library and had begun a long correspondence in which Auden gave him an informal course in literature. Auden was especially pleased to get him started on Kafka. He was equally helpful to unknown young poets who sent him their poems, offering detailed help on such technical matters as adjectives and enjambment.

When he felt obliged to stand on principle on some literary or moral issue, he did so without calling attention to himself, and he was impatient with writers like Robert Lowell whose political protests seemed to him more egocentric than effective. When he won the National Medal for Literature in 1967, he was unwilling either to accept it in Lyndon Johnson's White House during the Vietnam War or "to make a Cal Lowell gesture by a public refusal," so he arranged for the ceremony to be held at the Smithsonian, where he gave an acceptance speech about the corruption of language by politics and propaganda.

He was always professional in his dealings with editors and publishers, uncomplainingly rewriting whole essays when asked—except on at least two occasions when he quietly sacrificed money and fame rather than falsify his beliefs. In 1964, for his translation (with Leif Sjöberg) of Dag Hammarskjöld's posthumous *Markings*, he wrote a foreword that mentioned Hammarskjöld's "narcissistic fascination with himself" and alluded almost invisibly to Hammarskjöld's homosexuality, which Auden perceived as something entirely inward to Hammarskjöld and never acted upon:

> A "thorn in the flesh" which convinces him that he can never hope to experience what, for most people, are the two greatest joys earthly life has to offer, either a passionate devotion returned, or a lifelong happy marriage.

He also alluded to Hammarskjöld's inner sense of a messianic, sacrificial mission—something he seems to have recognized as a version of his own earlier temptations.

Auden had been Hammarskjöld's candidate for the Nobel Prize, and was widely expected to win it in 1964. Soon after Hammarskjöld's executors and friends saw Auden's typescript, he was visited by a Swedish diplomat who hinted that the Swedish Academy would be unhappy if it were printed in its present form, that perhaps it could be revised. Auden ignored the hint, and seems to have mentioned the incident only once, when he went to dinner with his friend Lincoln Kirstein the same evening and said, "There goes the Nobel Prize." The prize went to Jean-Paul Sartre, who refused it.

Two years later, *Life* magazine offered him ten thousand dollars for an essay on the fall of Rome, the last of a series by several authors titled "The Romans." Auden's typescript ended with his reflections on the fall of a later empire:

> I think a great many of us are haunted by the feeling that our society, and by ours I don't mean just the United States or Europe, but our whole world-wide technological civilisation, whether officially labelled capitalist, socialist or communist, is going to go smash, and probably deserves to.

The editors refused to inflict this on their patriotic mass-market readership in the era of the Pax Americana, and asked Auden to rewrite it. He declined, knowing that the piece would be dropped and that he would be paid nothing. Scholars knew for years that he had written the essay—an editor rescued it from the files when it was about to be discarded—but until recently no one seemed to know why it never appeared. Auden may have told the story only to one friend, Thekla Clark, who retold it in an interview about him nearly fifty years later.

Auden had many motives for portraying himself as rigid or uncaring when he was making unobtrusive gifts of time, money, and sympathy. In part he was reacting against his early fame as a leader and prophet, fame that now disgusted him because he saw the mixed motives behind his image of public virtue, the gratification he had felt in being idolized and admired. He felt degraded when asked to pronounce on political and moral issues about which, he reminded himself, artists had no special insight. Far from imagining that artists were superior to anyone else, he had seen in himself that artists have their own special temptations toward power and cruelty and their own special skills at masking their impulses from themselves.

Looking back at the crisis when Kallman ended their sexual relations and he reacted with murderous rage, he began to sense that he himself had caused the break between them by trying to reshape Kallman into an ideal figure, an imaginary lover whom he valued more than the real one. What Auden had thought of as a marriage of equals had been infected by *libido dominandi,* a lust for the power to transform the younger man into someone else. This was a temptation that everyone experienced, but artists, he thought, were especially susceptible to it. He said in a lecture on Shakespeare's sonnets: "Art may spill over from creating a world of language into the dangerous and forbidden task of trying to create a human being."

At the start of his career, when he half-hoped to make himself into a political poet, he made a conscious choice to write for a plural audience—that is, for a group or category of readers who, he wrote approvingly, "tended to have much the same interests and to see much the same things." He later realized that he had always preferred to write as if addressing an individual reader. He might have thousands of individual readers, but he wrote as if speaking to one. "All the poems I have written were written for love," he said; "naturally, when I have written one, I try to market it, but the prospect of a market played no role in its writing."

A writer who addresses a public, plural audience claims to deserve their collective attention. He must present himself as the great modernists—Yeats, Joyce, Eliot, Pound—more or less seriously presented themselves in relation to their culture, as visionary prophets, artist-heroes setting an agenda for their time and their nation. In contrast, a writer who addresses an individual reader presents himself as someone expert in his métier but in every other way equal with his reader, having no moral authority or special insight on anything beyond his art. Virginia Woolf, who thought much as Auden did about these matters, rebuked her readers for accepting an unequal relation with authors:

> In your modesty you seem to consider that writers are of different blood and bone from yourselves; that they know more of Mrs. Brown than you do. Never was there a more fatal mistake. It is this division between reader and writer, this humility on your part, these professional airs and graces on ours, that corrupt and emasculate the books which should be the healthy offspring of a close and equal alliance between us.

In an age when writers as different as Hemingway and Eliot encouraged their public to admire them as heroic explorers of the mind and spirit, Auden preferred to err in the opposite direction, by presenting himself as less than he was.

VI.

By refusing to claim moral or personal authority, Auden placed himself firmly on one side of an argument that pervades the modern intellectual climate but is seldom explicitly stated, an argument about the nature of evil and those who commit it.

On one side are those who sense in themselves what Auden called in a poem the "heart's invisible furies," evils they hope never to unleash, but which, as they sometimes perceive, add force to their ordinary angers and resentments, especially the angers they prefer to think are righteous. On the other side are those who can think of themselves without irony, "I am a good person," who perceive great evils only in other, evil people whose motives and actions are entirely unlike their own. This view has dangerous consequences when a party or nation, having assured itself of its inherent goodness, assumes its actions are therefore justified, even when, in the eyes of everyone else, they seem murderous and oppressive.

One of many forms this argument takes is a dispute over the meaning of the great totalitarian evils of the twentieth century: whether they reveal something about all of humanity or only about the uniquely evil leaders, cultures, and nations that committed them. For Auden, those evils made manifest the kinds of evil that were potential in everyone. Looking out from the attic room in peaceful, rural Austria where he composed his poems, he wrote (in "The Cave of Making"):

> More than ever
> life-out-there is goodly, miraculous, loveable,

but we shan't, not since Stalin and Hitler,
trust ourselves ever again: we know that, subjectively,
all is possible.

That is, "we"—all of us without exception—know what is possible "subjectively" in the mind of each one of us.

In "September 1, 1939" he dismissed the fantasy that anyone's private life could be innocent of the evils that so obviously drove public life. Individual persons know subjectively—as if looking in a mirror—that they treat others as objects to be used, just as nations do:

Out of the mirror they stare,
Imperialism's face
And the international wrong.

He observed to friends how common it was to find a dedicated antifascist who conducted his erotic life as if he were invading Poland.

Like everyone who thought more or less as he did, Auden didn't mean that erotic greeds were morally equivalent to mass murder or that there was no difference between himself and Hitler.* He was less interested in the obvious distinction between a responsible citizen and an evil dictator than he was in the more difficult question of what the citizen and dictator had in common, how the citizen's moral and psychological failures help the dictator to succeed.

Those who hold the opposite view, the view that the citizen and dictator have nothing in common, tend to hold many corollary views. One such corollary is that a suitable response to the vast evil of Nazi

---

*A complaint that someone else is asserting "moral equivalence" between one side and another is always an obfuscating distraction. Moral issues have nothing do with anything like "equivalence" that can be measured or counted.

genocide is wordless, uncomprehending awe—because citizen and dictator are different species with no language they can share. Another corollary view is that Hannah Arendt, in *Eichmann in Jerusalem,* a recurring flashpoint in this argument, was offensively wrong about the "banality of evil," because evil is something monstrous, exotic, and inhuman. The acts and thoughts of a good citizen, in this view, can be banal, not those of a dictator or his agents.

Auden revered Arendt; he wrote of her *The Human Condition* (1958) that it gave him "the impression of having been especially written for me"; he embarrassed her by proposing marriage when she was widowed in 1970; and he dedicated to her his last book, *Forewords and Afterwords* (1973). He had stated a view like hers about evil as early as 1939, in his poem "Herman Melville":

Evil is unspectacular and always human,
And shares our bed and eats at our own table.

He later quoted Simone Weil's *pensée* on the same theme, written around the same time: "Imaginary evil is romantic and varied; real evil is gloomy, monotonous, barren, boring."

The view that the citizen and dictator have nothing in common has another corollary: the view that the dictator's victims are inherently innocent, not merely innocent victims of someone else's evil, but innocent in everything, so that even after the murderous dictator has been destroyed, their own actions, no matter how oppressive or unjust, may not be judged by the same standard as his actions. As victims of irrational hatred, they cannot imagine themselves acting on comparable hatreds. Against this fantasy of inherent innocence, Auden recognized that victims, no matter how guiltless in their own victimization, are tempted to become victimizers in turn. As he put it briskly in a song, "Many a sore bottom finds / A sorer one to kick."

Auden took intellectual pleasure in sorting people into types and anti-types. Much of his work dramatizes a distinction between gentle-minded Arcadians, who dream of an innocent past where everyone could do as they wanted without harming anyone else, and stern-minded Utopians, who fantasize, and sometimes try to build, an ideal future in which all will act as they should. He identified himself as an Arcadian, but he never imagined that Utopians, no matter how much he disliked being around them, were solely to blame for public and private injustice, and he always reminded himself that Arcadians—who preferred to remain ignorant of other people's suffering—were not as innocent as they thought.

In "Under Which Lyre," his 1946 Harvard Phi Beta Kappa poem, he made a similar distinction under different names. Instead of Arcadians and Utopians, he described the unending war for the human heart between the playful children of Hermes the trickster and the authoritarian children of law-giving Apollo, and he urged his fellow irresponsibles to resist Apollo's battalions. But he told a friend afterward, "I have a bit of Apollo in me too." He later told another friend that he had authoritarian impulses in himself that he despised but could never entirely abolish. Even a committed Arcadian resorts to Utopian force when protecting his Eden:

> Liking one's Nature, as lake-lovers do, benign
> Goes with a wish for savage dogs and man-traps.

In Auden's prose poem "Vespers," an Arcadian and a Utopian unwillingly perceive that each shares in the guilt of their civilization, that each is responsible for the "cement of blood" without which "no secular wall will safely stand." When the two encounter each other at a crossroads, neither speaks, but each knows what the other thinks:

Both simultaneously recognize his Anti-type: that I am an
    Arcadian, that he is a Utopian.
He notes, with contempt, my Aquarian belly: I note, with
    alarm, his Scorpion's mouth.
He would like to see me cleaning latrines: I would like to see
    him removed to some other planet.

Far from responding to Nazi genocide with wordless awe, Auden
understood it as an extreme case of something all too comprehensible,
the pandemic fantasy of building New Jerusalem in the real world:

Even Hitler, I imagine, would have defined his New Jerusalem
as a world where there are no Jews, not as a world where they
are being gassed by the million day after day in ovens, but he
was a Utopian, so the ovens had to come in.

When Auden reviewed Isaiah Berlin's *The Hedgehog and the Fox*
in 1954, he offered an alternative to Berlin's antithesis of hedgehogs
who know one thing and foxes who know many. Improvising on
Alice in Wonderland, he contrasted strong-minded Alices, confident
in their moral rightness, with weak-minded Mabels, content to think
as everyone else thinks. His antithesis had more to do with moral
self-knowledge and its failures than with knowledge of the world.

Berlin was Auden's lifelong friend, and Auden was demurring gen-
tly at the Alice-like qualities he sensed in Berlin's book. One memorable statement of the Alice-like views that Auden mistrusted in
Berlin and himself occurs in Berlin's later essay on Turgenev. Berlin
wrote: "The dilemma of morally sensitive, honest, and intellectually
responsible men at a time of acute polarization of opinion has, since
[Turgenev's] time, grown acute and world-wide." Whatever Berlin

intended, a sentence like this encourages readers to count themselves among the sensitive, honest, and responsible, with the inevitable effect of blinding themselves to their own insensitivities, dishonesties, and irresponsibilities, and to the evils committed by a group, party, or nation that they support. Their "dilemma" is softened by the comforting thought of their merits.

Auden wrote a poem about complacency and its pleasures, pleasures that he knew he shared, though he had a sharp sense of their delusions. The poem was "Lakes" (1952):

> Only a very wicked or conceited man,
>   About to sink somewhere in mid-Atlantic,
> Could think Poseidon's frown was meant for him in person,
>   But it is only human to believe
> The little lady of the glacier lake has fallen
>   In love with the rare bather whom she drowns.

In the final stanza Auden wondered which kind of lake—"Moraine, pot, oxbow, glint, sink, crater, piedmont, dimple"—he would choose if he could own one, and ended on an ironic note of complacent pleasure at knowing, like Berlin's fox, many things: "Just reeling off their names is ever so comfy." He first published the poem with no dedication; when he reprinted it a few months after reviewing *The Hedgehog and the Fox* he dedicated it "For Isaiah Berlin."

A few years before he died in 1973, Auden began to focus his attention on religious ritual, not for the magical excitement it had given him in childhood, but because its timeless language and ritual were a stay against the complacent egoism that favors whatever is contemporary with ourselves, whatever vocabulary we happen to understand. "The rite," he said, "is the link between the dead and the unborn. As such, it requires a timeless language which, in practice, means a dead language." He wrote this in the context of the liturgical reforms of the 1960s and 1970s, to which he responded privately in a characteristic way. When the rector at Saint Mark's in-the-Bowery asked for his help on an experimental modernized liturgy, Auden spent hours discussing and revising it. Then, when Saint Mark's actually began using a new liturgy, Auden quietly began attending a Greek Orthodox and a Russian Orthodox church nearby, where the liturgy was still in Koine Greek or Old Church Slavonic, in which he did not know a single word. He chose to join a ritual that linked him to the remote past and the unknowable future, but only after he had helped his neighbor.

8

CELEBRANT: FRANK O'HARA

I.

FRANK O'HARA WAS the most sociable of poets, always happy to read aloud at parties, always praising friends or lovers or anyone else who got his attention, almost always portraying his inner life as if it existed only so that it could savor his outer one. O'Hara loved writers, artists, poems, paintings, bars, cafés, food, sex, film stars, buildings, and much else, and he seemed to toss them all into the mixed salads of his poetry with the same indifference to form and logic, the same domesticated surrealism, that characterized much of the American avant-garde of the 1950s and 1960s. Almost everyone who remembers O'Hara from his heady days in bohemian New York remembers him as the liveliest guest at any party in Greenwich Village or the Hamptons where the artistic and literary avant-garde gathered to celebrate itself.

But O'Hara was trying to find something different from what most of the other party guests were looking for, something far more sober, lonely, and serious. The best of the hundreds of poems that he wrote from around the age of twenty-three, in 1949, until his death at forty, in 1966, after a Jeep accident on a Fire Island beach, were private conversations with individual readers, too quiet to be heard in a crowded room. O'Hara wrote a seriously joking prose piece, "Personism: A Manifesto," that pretended to treat his poetic manner as an exciting avant-garde movement "which will undoubtedly have lots of adherents." Thanks to this new movement, he wrote, "the poem is at last between two persons instead of two pages." For a while, O'Hara also enjoyed writing showy, extravagant party pieces —long poems filled with miscellaneous names, places, and events— but his career began and ended with his shorter, deeper, more finely crafted lyrics, and the word "love" occurs more often in his shorter poems than in his longer ones.

No one who enjoyed O'Hara's avid presence at the avant-garde's crowded parties seems to have noticed that the jokes, gossip, and wild associative leaps in his poetry tended to culminate in sermons about the ultimate value of one-to-one relations. "The only truth is face to face," he wrote in "Ode: Salute to the French Negro Poets," a poem partly about the prejudicial falsehoods that blur individual faces. The closing couplet reads:

> the only truth is face to face, the poem whose words become
>   your mouth
> and dying in black and white we fight for what we love, not are

For O'Hara a poem was truthful when it was personal, not in the self-regarding "confessional" style of Robert Lowell's poems, which O'Hara called "just plain bad," but in the way in which one person attends to another: the words, in some way that defies definition, "become your mouth." What was worth fighting for was "what we love," not identity, essence, principles, blackness, whiteness, or anything else we might imagine defining what we are.

O'Hara made his living as a curator at the Museum of Modern

Art and as a reviewer for art magazines. The artworks he most admired were pictures of individual persons painted with the uniquely personal brushstrokes of painters such as Willem de Kooning and Larry Rivers. He disliked the flat, impersonal, mechanical images silkscreened by Andy Warhol and Roy Lichtenstein. But he was mostly too generous-minded to persist in his distaste or to use his influence against artists whom at first he disliked. He eventually wrote of one of Warhol's portraits that it was "not sarcastic... not some sort of stunt," as he had expected, but "absolutely moving and beautiful."

II.

O'Hara rushed into print with reviews and essays about the painters he wanted to celebrate and promote, but he resisted most opportunities to publish his poems. Aside from a few pamphlets printed by art galleries in tiny editions, he allowed only two collections to appear in his lifetime, *Meditations in an Emergency* (1957) and *Lunch Poems* (1964). Both had to be dragged out of him by their publishers; the second required six years of persuasion by Lawrence Ferlinghetti before O'Hara supplied the contents.

Any writer whose work is published mostly after his death gets his reputation shaped by other people. O'Hara's poems seemed so miscellaneous, so untethered to any career-shaping agenda, that the apparent shape of his work was left to be sculpted by his posthumous editors, who inevitably had agendas of their own. All posthumous editions of O'Hara's work are compiled mostly from poems that O'Hara never intended to publish.

Donald Allen, the energetic anthologist of the avant-garde who had helped get *Lunch Poems* into print, put everything he could find into the thick *Collected Poems* that appeared in 1971, five years after

O'Hara's death; a revised edition appeared in 1995. Allen also published a few further volumes containing poems that had eluded him in 1971, and he edited a *Selected Poems* in 1974. These are the books that formed the O'Hara that almost everyone remembers.

Mark Ford's selection in 2008 presents a different O'Hara from Allen's in 1974. The differences begin on the front covers. The older book displays Larry Rivers's nude portrait of O'Hara, with the genitals in brighter light and sharper focus than the face. The newer book displays a friend's photograph of O'Hara's face in profile, its expression contemplative and alert. Ford's selection makes it possible to see more clearly how inward O'Hara's poetry was at its best, and his version of O'Hara is more celebratory than Allen's, less eager to shock. Among O'Hara's longer poems, both Allen and Ford include the later "Ode to Michael Goldberg ('s Birth and Other Births)" and "Biotherm (for Bill Berkson)," which have much to say about hope, liberty, wine, and dessert. But Allen includes, and Ford omits, the earlier long poems "Hatred" and "Easter," which say a lot about excrement and pain.

The best books about O'Hara are Marjorie Perloff's critical study, *Frank O'Hara: Poet Among Painters* (1977, revised 1998), and Brad Gooch's biography, *City Poet: The Life and Times of Frank O'Hara* (1993). Both have titles that locate O'Hara in a group or a scene—in much the same way that the nude portrait on the old *Selected Poems* locates him in a collective sexual category—although both books are sensitive to the privacy and inwardness of O'Hara's best work. Gooch repeatedly observes that O'Hara wrote most fluently when he was alone, and that the densely populated world of his most public poems was his defense against an emptiness that both tempted and terrified him.

O'Hara was explicit about this temptation, and about the failure of his usual defenses against it, in a poem called "Anxiety":

I'm having a real day of it.
There was
something I had to do. But what?
There are no alternatives
Just the one something.
I have a drink,
it doesn't help—far from it!

A few lines later he wishes he could become "really dark, richly dark, like / being drunk," but even that would be second-best to the suicidal relief that a total dissolution into emptiness could bring:

the impossible
pure light, to be as if above a vast
prairie, rushing and pausing over
the tiny golden heads in deep grass.

Among O'Hara's contemporaries, few poets seem less like him than the repressed, unsociable, provincial English librarian Philip Larkin. But O'Hara's "Anxiety" has the same tone, mood, and plot of Larkin's "High Windows," in which all comforts seem impossible, and Larkin's anxiety issues finally in

the thought of high windows:
The sun-comprehending glass,
And beyond it, the deep blue air, that shows
Nothing, and is nowhere, and is endless.

O'Hara sometimes compared himself with the writers and artists among his friends, always insisting that he attempted less than they did—in a way that suggests that he was trying to suppress his sense that he achieved more. In one typically self-denigrating letter he wrote: "Where Kenneth [Koch] and Jimmy [James Schuyler] produce art, for instance, I often feel I just produce the by-product of exhibitionism." In the same letter, however, he recognized his deeper motives: "Sometimes I think that writing a poem is such a moral crisis I get completely sick of the whole situation." He served the cause of friendship by resisting his belief that his friends' desire to "produce art"—to confront an aesthetic crisis instead of a moral one—was their limitation.

Even his most comic and arbitrary-sounding poems tend to be essays on moral crises. The point of the comedy was not to dismiss the issues, but to disclaim any importance for himself in comparison with the issues. O'Hara's characteristic tone in his love poetry was that of unrequited passion (he seems never to have believed that he was loved in return by a man he fell in love with), as in an early poem, "Poetry," where his desire to be forever with his art is indistinguishable from his desire to be forever with a person:

All this I desire. To
deepen you by my quickness and delight
as if you were logical and proven,
but still be quiet as if
I were used to you; as if
you would never leave me
and were the inexorable
product of my own time.

And in one of his last poems, "Cantata," the closing lines about his orange cat are equally about someone human:

... he looks like my best friend my constant lover
hopelessly loyal tawny and apt and whom I hopelessly love

W. H. Auden famously warned O'Hara against the arbitrary, surrealistic shifts of tone and subject in the poems that he and his friend John Ashbery were writing in the 1950s:

> I think you (and John, too, for that matter) must watch what is always the great danger with any "surrealistic" style, namely of confusing authentic non-logical relations which arouse wonder with accidental ones which arouse mere surprise and in the end fatigue.

Auden, disliking both aesthetic and moral illogic, didn't perceive the almost opposite motivations behind the "non-logical relations" in O'Hara's poetry on the one hand and Ashbery's on the other. Ashbery's work, O'Hara said, "is full of dreams and a kind of moral excellence and kind sentiments," while his own "is full of objects for their own sake" that he treats with "ironically intimate observation." But Ashbery's dreamlike sentiments link together whatever happens to be in his mind while he is writing a poem, while O'Hara's "objects for their own sake" are linked together by his sense that, as in Dante's Paradise, everything that has profound value in itself is obscurely but profoundly connected to everything else that has similar value.

In O'Hara's best poems, the apparently non-logical relations in fact have a logic of their own. O'Hara was a lapsed Roman Catholic who detached himself cleanly and almost guiltlessly from his religious past. He lost all interest in Catholic theology and morals, but retained an aesthetic sensibility in which saints, shrines, relics, and rituals from wildly different centuries and cultures exist in a single harmonious texture of mutual adoration and love. The abrupt leaps from one object or person to another may look like the arbitrary leaps in Ashbery's poetry, but they have a logic founded in a Catholic sensibility that persisted after O'Hara discarded Catholicism.

When O'Hara links together a film star, a ballerina, a poet, and a half-dozen friends, he is being more Dantesque than surrealistic. In Canto II of the *Inferno*, when Virgil tells Dante they will journey together through Hell, Purgatory, and Paradise, Dante asks why someone as unheroic as he should be chosen. But heroism is irrelevant to grace; what matters is that other souls care about Dante's soul. Virgil explains that Mary (from first-century Nazareth) asked Lucia (from third-century Syracuse) to ask Beatrice (from thirteenth-century Florence) to ask Virgil (from first-century BC Rome) to come to his aid. They all exist for each other and for Dante, in more or less the same way that the friends, singers, and actors in O'Hara's poems exist for him and for each other.

O'Hara's most memorable poems are his elegies—"To My Dead Father," "To an Actor Who Died," "Thinking of James Dean," "The Day Lady Died"—and memorial poems such as "Ode on Causality," titled in an early draft "Ode at the Grave of Jackson Pollock." Modern elegies tend to be unconvincing because the poet so clearly disbelieves in the immortality that an elegy traditionally claims for its subject. But O'Hara's elegies succeed because, long after he discarded any religious belief in immortality, he retained the aesthetic sensibility that took it seriously. His best-known poem, "Lana Turner Has Collapsed!" (the tabloid headline that prompted the poem), is no less an elegy because its subject remained alive. The snowstorm in its opening lines is the sign of nature's conventionally elegiac grief. And its closing line offers the same collective praise—"Who would not sing for Lycidas?"—and evokes the same drama of resurrection and ascent—"So Lycidas sunk low, but mounted high"—that marks the climax of all great elegies:

oh Lana Turner we love you get up

One of the exercises he assigned to a young man who was trying to learn poetry from him was to read "Lycidas" and look up the allusions in Bullfinch's *Mythology*.

O'Hara's friends were dismayed by the camp sentimentality of his lesser elegies for James Dean, but these too recalled the fellowship of saints that presided over his childhood:

> This is
> James Dean, Carole Lombard. I hope
> you will be good to him up there.

In "Biotherm (for Bill Berkson)," O'Hara honored the "poète américain / lyrique et profond, Wallace Stevens," the source of Ashbery's aesthetic, the great poet who made connections among things because they were all present in his own imagination. But O'Hara wanted more than Stevens could give him. "I don't get any love from Wallace Stevens no I don't," he continued in the same poem, and then imagined Stevens isolated even in a crowd, superior to the surrounding mass, as he

> strolled on
> an ordinary evening alone
> with a lot of people

Politics, for most of O'Hara's avant-garde friends, was at best a target for dismissive satire, but O'Hara took politics seriously as a means to achieve social justice. Amiri Baraka recalled that he "had a real feeling for the human element in politics." As Brad Gooch reports in his biography, O'Hara got his news from the *Daily Worker* when he was young, and later puzzled his New York friends by taking the trouble to campaign for liberal candidates. He also puzzled his fellow guests at artistic house parties in the Hamptons by spending hours on the beach playing with his hosts' children, whom everyone else ignored.

III.

O'Hara was born in 1926 to observant Roman Catholic parents from small-town Massachusetts who never told him he had been conceived three months before they married. He hated his Catholic schools but brought away from them his special sensitivity to rhetoric and language. "To the Film Industry in Crisis" is a hagiography of film stars written in vaguely hexameter verse that opens, like Horace's *Carmina* 1.7, by listing the things he is not going to sing about:

> Not you, lean quarterlies and swarthy periodicals
> with your studious incursions toward the pomposity of ants,
> nor you, experimental theatre in which Emotive Fruition
> is wedding Poetic Insight perpetually, nor you,
> promenading Grand Opera, obvious as an ear (though you
> are close to my heart), but you, Motion Picture Industry,
> it's you I love!

Marjorie Perloff and others have catalogued O'Hara's debts to the avant-garde of early-twentieth-century Europe, but O'Hara's avant-garde credentials tend to obscure his uniqueness. Everyone in the mid-century American avant-garde knew how to copy Parisian experiments made forty years earlier, and the results were usually trivial and derivative. What made O'Hara's avant-garde-sounding poems different, and almost always rescued them from triviality and pretentiousness, was the classical and formal sensibility with which he held together all his avant-garde effects. In the same way, O'Hara was happy to imitate Charles Olson's phrases scattered on an open "field" or William Carlos Williams's long lines broken into three or four steps extending across the page ("blabbing along chicly while sitting on WC Williams' cracker barrel," he said in a letter), but his tone and language remained unmistakably his own.

After three years in the Pacific as a sonar operator for the navy during World War II, O'Hara went to Harvard on the GI Bill, found his personal voice as a poet, and discovered the excitement of working among an avant-garde coterie of poets, playwrights, and musicians. Until his Harvard years he expected to have a career as a concert pianist, and much of his verse has the kind of metrical dexterity found only among poets with a strong musical sense. "October" is an early display of the subtle variations he could make on a trimeter line:

If I turn down my sheets
children start screaming through
the windows. My glasses
are broken on the coffee table.
And at night a truce
with Iran or Korea seems certain
while I am beaten to death
by a thug in a back bedroom.

"Cohasset" is a later instance of his control over meter, as in the spondees that end the lines about stasis, followed by the trochee and dactyl in the closing lines about change:

the huge rocks
are like twin beds
and the cove tide
is a rug slipping
out from under us

Even when he is most intent on saying something about personal relations, his verse seems motivated partly by his love of language and form. "Aus einem April" is a variation on Rilke's poem with the same title. The shape of O'Hara's poem on the page is an exact match for the irregular shape of Rilke's poem, and O'Hara's opening line, "We dust the walls," is a joke rendering of Rilke's opening line, "*Wieder duftet der Wald* [the forest is fragrant again]," as it might look to an English-speaker who knew no German.* But the overall argument of O'Hara's poem seems to be that Rilke was interested only in the aesthetic sensations he got from a budding tree while O'Hara sees it as a sign of sympathy and feeling:

Haven't you ever fallen down at Christmas
        and didn't it move everyone who saw you?
            isn't that what the tree means? the pure pleasure
of making weep those whom you cannot move by your flights!

O'Hara tended to write two kinds of poem: short poems of about twenty to forty lines, with beginnings, middles, and ends, and longer poems that continued until he stopped. The shorter poems tend to be

---

*Fifteen years after O'Hara used this joke in one brief line, Celia and Louis Zukofsky extended the same technique—in complete seriousness—through a whole book of renderings from Latin, *Catullus* (1969). O'Hara had a better sense of when a trick gets tiresome, and he also managed to make his one-liner combine a linguistic joke and a typographical one: in German Fraktur type the *f* in *duftet* looks like a variant form of *s*.

reticent, psychologically acute love poems about the shifting inequal-
ities of love:

> out and out meanness, too, lets love breathe
> you don't have to fight off getting in too deep
> you can always get out if you're not too scared
>
> an ounce of prevention's
> enough to poison the heart
> don't think of others
> until you have thought of yourself, are true
>
> all of these things, if you feel them
> will be graced by a certain reluctance
> and turn into gold
>
> if felt by me, will be smilingly deflected
> by your mysterious concern
> ("Poem: Hate is only one of many responses")

The longer poems tend to be performance pieces, in which O'Hara
writes as a poetic one-man band, shifting rapidly among his roles as
party-goer, art critic, movie fan, amateur chef, balletomane, racon-
teur, sexual adventurer, European traveler, always rushing someplace
else, quick to shed his past, "capitalizing on a few memories / from
childhood by forgetting them." O'Hara's most frequent and most
ostentatiously avant-garde effects occur in these longer poems:

> whither Lumumba whither oh whither Gauguin
> I have often tried to say goodbye to strange fantoms I
> read about in the newspapers and have always succeeded

though the ones at "home" are dependent on Dependable
Laboratory and Sales Company on Pulaski Street strange
> ("For the Chinese New Year & for Bill Berkson")

In a talk he gave to a gathering of artists, O'Hara justified this
style of poetry as a liberation of language:

> Poetry which liberates certain forces in language, permits them
> to emerge upon the void of silence, not poetry which seeks
> merely to express most effectively or most beautifully or most
> musically some preconceived idea or perception.

For O'Hara this was an untypically conventional burst of avant-
garde apologetics. He generally cared more about the liberation of
human beings than of artistic media, and he knew perfectly well that
no poetry worth reading "seeks merely" to express a preconceived
idea. What O'Hara did in his longer poems under the banner of
language-liberation extended the techniques of earlier poets such as
Milton and Blake, who were equally willful in using names and images with resonant meanings for the poets themselves, meanings at
which a reader could marvel without fully comprehending them:

> Besides what the grim wolf with privy paw
> Daily devours apace, and nothing said;
> But that two-handed engine at the door
> Stands ready to smite once, and smite no more.
> > (Milton, "Lycidas")

> For Golgonooza cannot be seen till having pass'd the Polypus
> It is viewed on all sides round by a Four-fold Vision.
> > (Blake, "Milton")

O'Hara's obvious pleasure in writing these longer poems is mixed with a sense of strain at keeping the kaleidoscopic spectacle moving over hundreds of lines of verse. Public performance, no matter how much of his time he spent doing it, was not his natural medium—as he seems to have suggested in "Meditations in an Emergency":

It is easy to be beautiful; it is difficult to appear so.

IV.

One crucial difference between O'Hara and his great predecessors was that they wrote their most willfully arbitrary verse in response to their own private visions, while O'Hara seems to have written the willfully arbitrary verse of his longer poems partly to entertain his avant-garde friends. Verse written to entertain a public—Byron's *Don Juan,* for example—can be very great poetry, but it succeeds only when its inner logic is shared by both poet and reader.

A comic motif in Brad Gooch's biography of O'Hara is the eagerness with which members of the New York avant-garde endured the pretentious tedium of so many performances, readings, and exhibitions, so that they could feel (as one participant remembered) "proud to have been part of what we all thought was a deeply avant-garde production." When O'Hara wrote to entertain his avant-garde circle, he was not so much sharing with them an inner artistic logic as giving them the means to congratulate themselves for being avant-garde.

He joked in public about their conviction that anything avant-garde was inherently praiseworthy. When two of his friends decided to get married, he wrote a poem that praised them for doing something excellent—which therefore must be avant-garde, because the avant-garde is synonymous with excellence:

> It's so
>
> original, hydrogenic,* anthropomorphic, fiscal, post-anti-es-
> thetic, bland, unpicturesque and WilliamCarlosWilliamsian!
> it's definitely not 19th Century, it's not even Partisan Review,
> it's new, it must be vanguard!
>
> ("Poem Read at Joan Mitchell's")

Avant-gardes claim to create the art of the future. But the "art of the future" always proves wrong about the real future of art in the same way that the "city of the future" on display at a world's fair proves wrong about the future of cities. O'Hara's praise of some experimental poems by John Ashbery has a sharp double edge: "I might have known as I sink into the mush of love you would be foraging ahead into the 21st century."

Baudelaire dismissed the avant-garde as a "military metaphor"; until the mid-nineteenth century the word meant only the front ranks of an army. The avant-garde idea, he said, was suitable only to those "who can only think collectively" ("qui ne peuvent penser qu'en so-ciété")—not to those for whom, like O'Hara at his best, the only truth is face to face. An avant-garde coterie always prefers a revolution in language and technique to a revelation of thought and feeling. O'Hara recognized this preference as a sign of insecurity, a failure of nerve:

> it is the great period of Italian art when everyone imitates Picasso
> afraid to mean anything

Membership in a coterie, school, or group produces different effects on major and minor writers. For minor writers, a group pro-

---

* "Hydrogenic," like "Biotherm" in one of O'Hara's titles, is a word he seems to have found on a cosmetics label.

vides a repertory of styles and themes and gives them confidence to work at the height of their powers. They return the favor by compiling group anthologies and writing manifestos, but when the group disintegrates, they may have nothing more to say. For major writers, a group tends to provide themes and publicity in the first few years of their career, when they are already looking elsewhere, and their mature work has nothing in common with the later work of the rest of the group. The members left behind, now famous mostly because they had once been associated with the major writer, mutter resentfully that he betrayed them.

O'Hara was a major writer who tried to convince himself he was a minor one. His best work either ignored or teased the coterie he partied with, but as he grew older he found it easier to fight off loneliness by immersing himself in an always-welcoming group than by opening himself to the risks of any intimacy that might relieve it.* In the last years of his life, his closest friends found it difficult to break through the wall of young acolytes that closed around him at bars and parties, deepening his unhappiness. Their youth and beauty promised him long-awaited satisfactions, while their emotional and intellectual inequality made satisfaction impossible. Liquor masked the resulting frustration and pain. The more time O'Hara spent bar-hopping with his coterie, the fewer poems he wrote, and the more convinced he became that he had nothing more to say.

The last poem he wrote, four months before he died, proves that he was mistaken. "Little Elegy for Antonio Machado"—the twentieth-century Spanish poet whose early avant-garde affinities and later political and moral passions were not unlike O'Hara's—is not little

---

* Two thoughtful and well-informed books take a far more positive view of O'Hara's connections with his group: Andrew Epstein, *Beautiful Enemies: Friendship and Postwar American Poetry* (Oxford University Press, 2006), and Lytle Shaw, *Frank O'Hara: The Poetics of Coterie* (University of Iowa Press, 2006).

as its title claims, but compressed, dark, and magnificent, with a depth and directness that fulfill the promise of O'Hara's earlier lyrics. He devised for it a regular form that looks like a Horatian stanza that someone broke and put together again without quite restoring the original. The poem is another of O'Hara's elegies in which both mourner and mourned are glorified by their recognition of the darknesses they share and the light they aspire to:

> your water air and earth
> insist on our joining you
> in recognition of colder prides and less negotiable ambitions

As the elegy ends, he imagines Machado reviving like the heroes of other elegies, but also "improving" O'Hara and ourselves in the physically direct way that salt improves a meal:

> improving your soul's expansion
> in the night and developing our own in salt-like praise

By chance or by luck, the last word of O'Hara's last poem names the action that drove his whole career.

A NOTE ON SOURCES

Earlier versions of these chapters appeared in *The New York Review of Books,* as follows:

"The Demonic Trilling," June 7, 2012.

"Dwight, the Passionate Moralist," March 8, 2012.

"New York Everyman," June 12, 2008, and "The Hidden Life of Alfred Kazin," August 18, 2011.

"The Perils of His Magic Circle," April 29, 2010.

"The Obedient Bellow," April 28, 2011, and "Old Saul and Young Saul," September 26, 2013.

"The Strange Powers of Norman Mailer," November 21, 2013.

"Auden and God," December 6, 2007, and "The Secret Auden," March 20, 2014.

"'What We Love, Not Are,'" September 25, 2008.

A few sentences in the introduction are adapted from "The Myths of Christopher Isherwood," December 19, 2013.

EDWARD MENDELSON is the Lionel Trilling Professor in the Humanities at Columbia University and the literary executor of the Estate of W. H. Auden. His books include *The Things That Matter*— about seven novels by Mary Shelley, Charlotte and Emily Brontë, George Eliot, and Virginia Woolf—and *Early Auden* and *Later Auden*. He has edited novels by Arnold Bennett, Thomas Hardy, George Meredith, Anthony Trollope, and H. G. Wells, and has written for *The New York Review of Books*, *The Times Literary Supplement*, the *London Review of Books*, *The New York Times Book Review*, *The New Republic*, and many other publications.